Parenting Teens

How to Be the Best Mom and Dad at the Same Time

(Newborn to Year One, Steps on Your Infant to Toddler)

William Velez

Published by Rob Miles

© William Velez

All Rights Reserved

Parenting Teens: How to Be the Best Mom and Dad at the Same Time (Newborn to Year One, Steps on Your Infant to Toddler)

ISBN 978-1-990084-28-7

All rights reserved. No part of this guide may be reproduced in any form without permission in writing from the publisher except in the case of brief quotations embodied in critical articles or reviews.

Legal & Disclaimer

The information contained in this book is not designed to replace or take the place of any form of medicine or professional medical advice. The information in this book has been provided for educational and entertainment purposes only.

The information contained in this book has been compiled from sources deemed reliable, and it is accurate to the best of the Author's knowledge; however, the Author cannot guarantee its accuracy and validity and cannot be held liable for any errors or omissions. Changes are periodically made to this book. You must consult your doctor or get professional medical advice before using any of the suggested remedies, techniques, or information in this book.

Upon using the information contained in this book, you agree to hold harmless the Author from and against any damages, costs, and expenses, including any legal fees potentially resulting from the application of any of the information provided by this guide. This disclaimer applies to any damages or injury caused by the use and application, whether directly or indirectly, of any advice or information presented, whether for breach of contract, tort, negligence, personal injury, criminal intent, or under any other cause of action.

You agree to accept all risks of using the information presented inside this book.

You need to consult a professional medical practitioner in order to ensure you are both able and healthy enough to participate in this program.

Table of Contents

INTRODUCTION 1

CHAPTER 1: YOU KEEP MAKING EXCUSES 3

CHAPTER 2: BEING A PARENT AT EVERY STAGE OF YOUR CHILD'S LIFE 13

CHAPTER 4: CHILDREN OF DESTINY 23

CHAPTER 5: KEEPING KIDS BUSY AND SAFE DURING ROAD TRIPS 37

CHAPTER 6: ARE TANTRUMS BENEFICIAL FOR YOUR TODDLERS? 41

CHAPTER 7: INTO THE WORLD OF A YOUNG TEENAGER .. 49

CHAPTER 8: FEELINGS OF DYSLEXIC CHILD 60

CHAPTER 9: UNDERSTAND THE DIFFERENCES BETWEEN MOTHERHOOD AND FATHERHOOD 70

CHAPTER 10: FOUNDATION OF PARENTING 90

CHAPTER 11: IF IT DOESN'T WORK, CHANGE IT 110

CHAPTER 12: A POSITIVE APPROACH TO CHANGING CHILDREN'S BEHAVIORS 121

CHAPTER 13: SELF-WORTH AND SELF-AWARENESS 130

CHAPTER 14: 4 STEPS TO HELP YOUR VIDEO GAME "ADDICTED" CHILD 138

CHAPTER 15: TRAIN YOUR CHILD AT AN EARLY AGE 142

CHAPTER 16: TIPS ON AWARENESS 149

CHAPTER 17: ROLE OF COMMUNICATION IN HANDLING TEEN KIDS 153

CHAPTER 18: TRANSITION TO ELEMENTARY SCHOOL FOR YOUR CHILD 157

CHAPTER 19: DO NOT OVERSTEP YOUR BOUNDS 162

CHAPTER 20: NEWBORN TO 23 MONTHS 168

CHAPTER 21: POSITIVE PARENTING WITH TEENAGERS .. 188

CONCLUSION 199

Introduction

What's with parents and losing their temper when their children become disobedient? This is a common occurrence in most households. Did you know that the shouting and yelling that results from losing your temper does not have a positive effect on your child but rather makes them to be even more rebellious towards you? As a parent, it is very demoralizing when you find yourself having to enter into arguments and fights with your child. The act of administering discipline to your child can be very annoying and overwhelming at the same time. In a society where careers consume most of the parents time, the act of effective discipline is lost. By reading this book, you will be introduced to a mindful way of disciplining your child with less effort on your part by use of Zen Habits hence you will end up being a good parent as well as see your child grow into a responsible adult.

I would urge you to read this book and borrow a leaf or two on how to instill a sense of discipline and responsibility in your child through mindful parenting.

Chapter 1: You Keep Making Excuses

During a play date you cringe and tell your friend for the thousandth time "Lisa's just tired," as she throws herself to the floor in a fit of rage over the Twizzler she was denied. Billy's 'schedule is just off since summer has started' and Chrissy is 'going through a phase' or 'just has an attitude problem today.'

Congratulations, you've given your friend nothing but an excuse to your child's behavior (instead of a consequence) and your child permission to continue displaying their unwanted behavior. Do children have 'off' days? Absolutely. Does this off day have precedence over how your child responds to directives? Absolutely not.

To be clear, an excuse is an explanation that justifies a fault. In other words, your child's tantrum/screaming fit/outright refusal to abide is given the 'A-Okay' by parents every time an excuse is made (or overheard by your child). Now if you had perfectly angelic offspring you wouldn't be reading this, so enough chatter, let's dive in.

Why you B*tch: Let's be honest; it's time consuming and embarrassing when your child has a complete meltdown in the middle of the bank. Or the park. Or church. You probably feel as though you have set up all environmental factors to be ideal for this particular outing, so you're at a total loss when a denial to 'One more time down the slide' or 'Can I have a lollipop from the bank teller' results in the apocalypse of breakdowns. Instead of issuing a consequence, you excuse the behavior and vow to bring up their behavior at a more convenient time or setting.

Some things you may be B*tching about include: "I don't understand why he/she does this", "This happens every time we decide to go out" and "That's it, I guess we can't go out as a family anymore if Bobby is going to act like this."

Why the problem exists: Any time an excuse is made you are giving the child permission to continue on with their behavior. By not actively issuing a consequence to an undesired behavior you become complicit in the way they act. Maybe you knew that already. What you may not realize is that when you vocally explain or justify a child's French fry throwing antics to a nearby adult to ease your own embarrassment, you are giving them ammo to use against you. Consider the below (true) scenario:

Parent: "Robin is just tired. She doesn't normally act like this."

Friend: "Oh, that's okay. Jim has days like that too."

Parent: "Yeah I don't think she slept well. She acts like this around people to show off too."

Friend: "I understand, it's okay."

Later on that evening...

Child: "Mom can I have a cookie?"

Parent: "With the way you were acting earlier? No way."

Child: "But Mom I was tired, I didn't sleep good. It won't happen again, please?"

See what happened there? Not only was the child in earshot of the adult excusing the behavior, thereby giving them a free pass, the child was then later able to use the same excuse against the parent to coax them into getting a treat later on in the day.

As human beings we are instinctively uncomfortable with being portrayed as having a conflict of opinions. The parent had suggested that the child was tired, so when the child used tiredness as an excusal to their behavior it only served as a validation to what the parent had already suggested. In case you were wondering, this client happened to be a 10 year old girl, and yes, she got the cookie.

How to start Parenting: If you can excuse your child's behavior as no big deal then there's no reason for it to be a big deal to a child. Making their behavior into a big deal, especially in public, makes them more conscious of their behavior and what behaviors you're expecting. Make the following changes every time you feel the urge to excuse their behavior:

1) Issue an age appropriate consequence, IMMEDIATELY, and STICK TO IT.

Not when you're in the car on the way home, or when you're in a secluded enough spot so you won't have other adults or people hear. Right then and there, issue your consequence: "If you do not lower your voice, we will not visit Grandma's later." Your child opposed to being disciplined in public? Well, then you better believe their attitude and behavior will change all the faster.

The thing to remember here: Stick to what you say, the very first time you say it. Don't issue a consequence to sound threatening or gain their attention if you don't mean it. Ever read The Boy Who Called Wolf? Same idea. Children learn to decipher when your threats are empty and it will put you back at square one.

2) Make the Child the 'Punisher' with a 'Not listening Jar'

Sit down with your child(ren) and talk about consequences that seem fair to them. This is important for two reasons: It lets them establish their own consequences and it doesn't put the punishment aspect on yourself or their caregiver if they were the ones who chose it in the first place.

For example, you might ask: "What would be a fair punishment for talking back?" and they might respond with something like "I can't play with my red truck" or "I have to clean my room." Maybe you were thinking of issuing consequences such as time out or no TV, which are also effective, but now you have two more very specific consequences to add to the jar that you know will work since they thought of them.

This can be a fun activity; decorate Popsicle sticks with consequences written on them. Mark a jar for each child or have three different levels of consequence jars depending on the severity of the behavior. You can even have separate jars for at home and in the car for outings.

*It is important that this activity be completed when both parent and child are mutually in happy moods and not in the midst of a crisis.

3) "Don't do that again." "Do what?" "That." "What's that?"

Owning up to their behavior is a must in any negative behavior/consequence scenario. If they don't understand why they are being punished, how are they supposed to learn to not display that behavior again? Consider the following prompt:

Parent: "Okay Charlie, the timer went off, before you get up why are you sitting in time out?"

Child: "I don't know."

Parent: "Would you like to sit in time out longer to think about it?"

Child: "No!"

Parent: "Okay, what did you do that made you get a time out?"

Child: "I hit Robbie."

Parent: "Is it okay to hit Robbie?"

Child: "No."

Parent: "What happens if you hit Robbie again?"

Child: "I go back in time out."

Notice how the parent changed the way they asked the child why they were in time out. Sometimes a child can get so upset while in trouble they may genuinely forget or not understand the question, at that point it would be acceptable to coach them to providing the answer (Ex: Who did you hit?). The important aspect of this is that the child voices their involvement in the negative behavior, they establish with you that it is unacceptable, and they realize that a repeat offense will put them back in the time out chair.

Chapter 2: Being A Parent At Every Stage Of Your Child's Life

Raising children is no simple task, and when you are a single mother, you must be prepared for some serious challenges. This does not mean you should feel anxious about it – as your baby takes its first steps and grows into an adult, you grow as a mother and that itself is an experience to be cherished.

To make single parenting less daunting, here are some tips to help you deal with the different phases of your child's growing years.

Early years: Baby to Toddlers

Accept the help of family if possible.

Having a newborn is quite exciting but exhausting at the same time. A newborn child needs emotional and financial attention. If you are new to the role of a mother, then you definitely need help.

Ask your mother, aunt, cousin or anyone else to stay with you for at least the first few weeks.

It will help you in a huge manner. You can even ask them to take turns in assisting you. If your family lives far away and is not available, seek assistance from your friends.

Join an online parenting group.

This will help you share and discuss your problems with other moms going through a similar experience as yours. You can even get in touch with married moms to discuss the needs of a newborn. This will help you find the right kind of support.

Don't neglect signs of postpartum depression.

Postpartum depression is common among new mothers. If your family or friends or you yourself see any signs of depression, consult a healthcare professional. It can be treated easily and will help you in a great manner. It will help in improving your holistic state of being.

Learn to let go of what is not so important.

When your baby is an infant, he/she will have a need to be fed regularly, cleaned, rocked and cared for. The other important thing is you should be able to take care of yourself by eating healthy and start doing light exercises.

Do not undermine your own value when taking care of the baby, as you are important too.

Try to socialize as much as you can, as mummyhood, especially single mummyhood is a difficult path. Socializing and mingling with people will help in addressing the stress.

Middle Years: Elementary/Middle School Age

Set your priorities.

This is the phase when your child will start picking up essential traits that will define his/her personality. As your child begins school, there will be responsibilities related to packing your kid's lunch, helping with the homework, keeping an eye on whom your child socializes with, etc. This will be in addition to your career and other household responsibilities. Set your priorities, and try to come up with a schedule so every responsibility is catered to.

Manage your child's behavior and inculcate discipline.

Put your child to sleep early and maintain a schedule. A good 9-10 hours of sleep will make your child more pliable. Also this will give you a break to relax and unwind. Get creative and think of ways you can make your child spend time on his/her own in an interesting manner. Some skill requiring games and toys would be of help. Encourage outdoor activities like soccer, basketball, cycling, etc.

Improve relations with neighbors.

Your neighbors are the first point of contact for you, in case of any problem. Whether you are leaving your child alone at home for long hours, or your child falls ill all of a sudden or any such emergency situation; your neighbors will prove helpful.

Teen Years: High School

Give your child space and respect their privacy.

A teenage child likes to feel responsible and grown up. Allow adequate space to let them develop their own personality. Let them explore new areas of interest and be supportive in all. Try to get them to discuss about their daily activities, so you know what they are up to. Rather than monitoring your child, act like a friend.

Draw a line to your leniency and let your child know your expectations

While being their friend, you have to simultaneously remember that it is your responsibility to keep your child from falling into bad company.

Tell them your parameters of acceptable behavior, set expectations and be open to discussion when making the terms.

Keep an eye on where they spend their money, monitor their internet usage, and their friend circles. If possible, keep in touch with some of their friends' parents. This is an age when they are easily influenced, so pay attention, so that they are influenced by the right kind of morals.

Make them work for a reward

Now your child is old enough to share some responsibilities in the house like laundry, preparing dinner, buying grocery etc. Offer them some rewards in return of successfully accomplishing these little jobs. Positive reinforcement works wonders in parenting.

Plan more activities with your child

Don't let the hours you are together at home be the only time you spend with your child. Go out for movies, lunch, sport events or shopping with your child. They need normalcy in their life and need to feel like a family.

Most single parents are unable to spend enough time with their kids, as they are busy making a living. This may lead to some kind of alleviation between the kid and you. Spending ample quality time with them will help you tackle that problem.

Youth/Adult: Going to College

Treat them as an adult

You may feel that your adult child is still a child, but now is the time to stop being over-protective. At this stage, your child may like to discuss their problems with their friends and spend more time with them.

Take that in your stride. Once in a while, it is good to guide if your child is undergoing a serious crisis. Otherwise, do not intrude too much, just let your child know you are there for them. They will feel comfortable sharing their problems with you when the time is right.

Encourage them to come up with ways to earn money.

It's high time your child begins some part time job to raise money for their personal expenditures. This way, they will also learn the art of money management. You do not need to keep a track of all the things that your child buys, but stay watchful if they get into drugs and alcohol.

Ask them to clean their own mess.

The living area of an adult child is a private space. Let them tidy it themselves and let them fix their little problems themselves.

Getting their broken gadgets fixed, getting a driving license etc. are now their responsibility, let them do it on their own.

Chapter 4: Children Of Destiny

Do you know what an awesome gift or treasure that baby you held in your arms is? Each child is a unique creation of God. Your child is a masterpiece, a one-off creation specially designed by God. Ephesians 2:10a, in the New Living Translation, says 'For we are God's masterpiece'. Before your child was conceived God formed your child to be a certain way, with a specific personality, disposition and interests. Your child is not here by mistake and her specific make up and tendencies are not by chance. God knew your child before He put him in your womb (or your wife's womb, if you are a dad) -Jeremiah 1:5 and formed him to be his unique self.

Not only is your child uniquely created, she is uniquely created for a purpose! Ephesians 2:10b, says, 'He has created us anew in Christ Jesus, so we can do the good things he planned for us long ago' God has a plan for his life and what he is going to be and do. Each child has a specific work on this earth and a divine mandate to fulfill.

When we have this insight into God's mind, that each child is uniquely crafted for a purpose; then we understand that each child is designed to be, and has the potential to be, exceptional. To be exceptional means to be uncommon, special, very good or peculiar.

When a child

• is given the education and life skills to succeed,

• is whole and happy,

- discovers his or her God given gifts, talents and calling,

- and is helped to develop and walk in it

– that child will be an exceptional child.

An Arrow

Psalm 127:4 describes our children as arrows. Most people know what the purpose of an arrow is - arrows are missiles designed to be shot to hit a target or a mark. Psalm27: 14 is thus revealing to us a key parenting insight - that each child is an arrow, to be shot at a specific direction or location. There is a target place for each child to get to, a destiny for each child and a specific path that each child is called to walk.

It is easy as parents to just see our children as sweet little things, reflections of us or a 'mini-me' - to be enjoyed (almost in the way one enjoys a pet), cuddled and pampered. Some others can see their children as burdens - nuisances or distractions that clog up their life and take up their time. We may never call them that, but deep in our hearts that is how we can see them at times – as time consuming, demanding, high investment and low return. However, this scripture makes it clear that each child is so much more than that – each child is a wonderful treasure, an arrow- designed to hit a mark, with a destiny to fulfill.

Jeremiah 29:11 confirms the idea of a targeted life when it states, '…I know the plans I have for you….', affirming that God has a plan for each person's life. The word 'plans' in Jeremiah 29:1 means "purpose" or "work". The word 'works' in Ephesians 2:10, which we looked at earlier in this chapter, means "labour, business, employment, that with which any one is occupied, that which one undertakes to do, an enterprise, undertaking". These word definitions further demonstrate that God has a purpose, a design, a pattern for each child's life – a work for them to do, a business or a task for them to undertake.

Let's look at a few bible stories, which demonstrate this, with God unveiling His plans for a child's life even before the child was born!

Samson's story

In the book of Judges, chapter 13, Samson's parents had an angelic visitation that made it clear to them that God had a plan for this child. Samson's purpose was to begin the process of delivering a nation from its oppressors.

2 There was a certain man of Zorah, of the tribe of the Danites, whose name was Manoah. And his wife was barren and had

no children. 3 And the angel of the Lord appeared to the woman and said to her, "Behold, you are barren and have not borne children, but you shall conceive and bear a son. 4 Therefore be careful and drink no wine or strong drink, and eat nothing unclean, 5 for behold, you shall conceive and bear a son. No razor shall come upon his head, for the child shall be a Nazirite to God from the womb, and he shall begin to save Israel from the hand of the Philistines." 6 Then the woman came and told her husband, "A man of God came to me, and his appearance was like the appearance of the angel of God, very awesome. I did not ask him where he was from, and he did not tell me his name, 7 but he said to me, 'Behold, you shall conceive and bear a son. So then drink no wine or strong drink, and eat nothing unclean, for the child shall be a Nazirite to

God from the womb to the day of his death."

John and Jesus's story

It wasn't only Samson's parents that angels visited with a message about the destiny of their child; much later angels would call on an old priest called Zechariah and a young woman called Mary to tell them about their children. These angelic visits are recorded in Luke 1. John's purpose was to lay the path for, and direct people to, Jesus.

And there appeared to him an angel of the Lord standing on the right side of the altar of incense. 12 And Zechariah was troubled when he saw him, and fear fell upon him. 13 But the angel said to him, "Do not be afraid, Zechariah, for your prayer has been heard, and your wife Elizabeth will bear you a son, and you shall call his name

John. 14 And you will have joy and gladness, and many will rejoice at his birth, 15 for he will be great before the Lord. And he must not drink wine or strong drink, and he will be filled with the Holy Spirit, even from his mother's womb. 16 And he will turn many of the children of Israel to the Lord their God, 17 and he will go before him in the spirit and power of Elijah, to turn the hearts of the fathers to the children, and the disobedient to the wisdom of the just, to make ready for the Lord a people prepared.

Jesus's purpose was to deliver the world from an eternity in hell and lead as many as receive Him, into a living relationship with God.

26 In the sixth month the angel Gabriel was sent from God to a city of Galilee named Nazareth, 27 to a virgin betrothed to a man whose name was Joseph, of the

house of David. And the virgin's name was Mary. 28 And he came to her and said, "Greetings, O favored one, the Lord is with you!" 29 But she was greatly troubled at the saying, and tried to discern what sort of greeting this might be. 30 And the angel said to her, "Do not be afraid, Mary, for you have found favor with God. 31 And behold, you will conceive in your womb and bear a son, and you shall call his name Jesus. 32 He will be great and will be called the Son of the Most High. And the Lord God will give to him the throne of his father David, 33 and he will reign over the house of Jacob forever, and of his kingdom there will be no end."

These three biblical examples confirm that God has plans for children even before they are born. Do you, as a parent, know what God's plan is for your child's life? If you don't, it is important that you discover it. Don't you wish an angel would just show up and make it clear what that purpose is, like in bible times? If only it were that easy! Thankfully we can inquire of God, like Rebecca did. Angels didn't visit her but she sensed she was carrying children of destiny and she asked God about their destiny. Her story is recorded in Genesis 25.

And Isaac prayed to the Lord for his wife, because she was barren. And the Lord granted his prayer, and Rebecca his wife conceived. 22 The children struggled together within her, and she said, "If it is thus, why is this happening to me?" So she went to inquire of the Lord. 23 And the Lord said to her,

"Two nations are in your womb, and two peoples from within you shall be divided; the one shall be stronger than the other, the older shall serve the younger."

Like Rebecca, you must begin to inquire about the destiny of your child or children. Seek God for understanding on this. We are not told how God revealed this to Rebecca, there is no mention of angels; but in some way, He communicated each child's destiny to their mother.

Warrior parenting

Samson's father's response is also instructive for us as parents. Once he discovered God had a purpose for his son. He wanted to know what part he had to play as a parent.

8 Then Manoah prayed to the Lord and said, "O Lord, please let the man of God whom you sent come again to us and teach us what we are to do with the child who will be born." 9 And God listened to the voice of Manoah, and the angel of God

came again to the woman as she sat in the field. But Manoah her husband was not with her. 10 So the woman ran quickly and told her husband, "Behold, the man who came to me the other day has appeared to me." 11 And Manoah arose and went after his wife and came to the man and said to him, "Are you the man who spoke to this woman?" And he said, "I am." 12 And Manoah said, "Now when your words come true, what is to be the child's manner of life, and what is his mission?" 13 And the angel of the Lord said to Manoah, "Of all that I said to the woman let her be careful. 14 She may not eat of anything that comes from the vine, neither let her drink wine or strong drink, or eat any unclean thing. All that I commanded her let her observe."

Judges 13

It is interesting that even though Samson was the deliverer, his parents were also given instructions on how to live. Samson's mother was instructed to abstain from wine and unclean things in order to raise a certain type of child. As parents, we are required to play a key role in the fulfilment of God's plan for our child's life. You have a part to play and a price to pay. To raise exceptional children requires exceptional parenting.

Raising exceptional children requires that you become a warrior for your children's destiny. A warrior is defined as a brave or experienced soldier or fighter. Like a warrior, you must be ready fight for your children's destiny and to bring experience and skill (yours or that borrowed from other exceptional individuals) to develop them into their full potential.

In chapter 3 we'll talk more about how we can discern Gods plan for each child, so that you can know how your arrow (child) is to be targeted; but first let's explore your role as a warrior in your child's life some more in the next chapter.

Chapter 5: Keeping Kids Busy And Safe During Road Trips

Road trips with children can be very challenging. The car is compact and there's not much space to move around. Children will certainly get bored and might throw tantrums along the way. So if you want to make this trip worthwhile and enjoyable for the whole family, follow these helpful tips…

"Spot the road sign" game

Print out all the road signs from the internet and laminate it. This will ensure that these road sign cards will last through the whole journey and will still be useful for future road trips. Give these cards to the kids and let them get one card at a time. They have to spot the road sign printed on the card. Each road sign they find is equivalent to a certain number of points. It can be converted to cash for their allowance or it can be in a form of a gift or stop-overs along the way or it can also be an opportunity for them to go on outing or camping trips. The kids will not only enjoy the journey, it will also give them an opportunity to get acquainted with different signs on the road. For parents, this means a road trip full of new discovery for kids and a journey that will be fun and tantrum-free.

Road-mysteryville

This game is quite similar to the spot the road sign game. The only difference is, the kids won't be spotting road signs. Instead, they will have to find the things listed on a sheet of paper. These things can be a gasoline station, an airplane, a motorcycle, a dump truck, a barn, a horse, a river, McDonald's restaurant or a bus. Make the list as creative and as many as possible. Once an item on the list is found, that item will have to be crossed out from the list and every item is equivalent to 1 point which; when accumulated can be converted to cash or exchanged for a gift or "free time".

Photo albums

Children who are still very young and are still unable to read will definitely love flipping through some old photos while on a road trip. They especially love to look through their own photos when they were still younger. While looking through some photos, make sure to supplement it with a story telling them when the picture was taken. The kids' curiosity will definitely fire up and will ask you so many questions that will surely keep them occupied through the whole journey.

Guessing games

Children naturally love to guess. So for every long trip, you have to incorporate a guessing game. Each has to think of an item and let the others guess what it is.

Chapter 6: Are Tantrums Beneficial For Your Toddlers?

According to recent research, dealing with toddler tantrums is the most challenging task for many parents. Most people will feel accomplished as parents whenever their children are at ease and smiling. However, the same parents will feel dismay when their children are rolling on the floor, throwing their tiny legs aimlessly, and whining incessantly.

However, the majority of parents don't understand that toddler tantrums are a critical part of the child's emotional wellbeing and health. For this reason, every parent should learn to be patient whenever the child is having tantrums. Let's look at some of the key reasons why your child's tantrum is beneficial.

· Better outside than inside

Tears comprise a stress hormone known as cortisol. When your child cries, he or she is getting rid of stress from the body. Tears are known to reduce blood pressure and enhance emotional health, so a parent must support the baby and facilitate emotional regulation. You may realize that when your child is about to throw tantrums, something must be wrong. Maybe they're frustrated, whining, or angry? You might have also discerned that after the experience, their mood improves. It's helpful if you allow your toddler's tantrum without interrupting to ensure they purge the bad feelings.

· Crying helps your child learn.

A few weeks ago, I was with my niece, who's five years. She was playing and began throwing tantrums because she got stuck. Nevertheless, after crying, she relaxed and figured out how to complete the task. I've experienced many cases where a toddler is struggling, and expressing one's frustrations can assist one to clear his or her minds and learn new things. Learning happens naturally to children. However, if the child can't focus or listen, there must be a possible emotional problem that blocks her progress. For a child to learn new things, she must be relaxed and happy, so uttering emotional upset is part of the procedure.

· Your child will sleep better.

Sleeping difficulties always happen since many parents believe that the ideal way to deal with tantrums is to prevent them. Then, the child's stifled emotions explode when the brain is resting. Like grown people, children lack sleep since they're stressed or attempting to digest something that's occurring in their lives. Letting your child complete the tantrums will improve her emotional health and will assist her stability.

· You refused them something, and it's a good thing.

A possibility is that your child is throwing tantrums since you said no to something he or she badly wanted. That is a good thing to do as a parent. Saying no offers your child a clear boundary about unacceptable and acceptable habits. In most cases, parents avoid saying no since they're often not ready to handle the emotional outburst. However, try to stand firm with your limits as you provide love, hugs, and empathy. Saying no to some stuff implies that you aren't afraid of the cluttered and emotional side of parenting.

· Your child will feel safe to express her feelings.

Tantrums can be a huge compliment even though it doesn't sound that way. In many cases, children don't use tantrums to manipulate parents to receive the things they need. Often, the child accepts the no, so tantrums are the expression of how he or she feels about it. While you stand firm with your decision, try to empathize with her sad state. If your child's upset about a broken cookie or the type of a toy, it's often a ploy to attain the attention and love she seeks.

· Tantrums can bring you closer together.

It might be difficult to believe at the moment but watch and wait. Your upset child might not seem like she likes to be with you at the moment, but she wants you. Let her overcome her challenges without you trying to help her. Never talk too much, but try to share some reassuring, empathetic, and kind words. Give your child hugs. The child will soak up your unconditional love and feel close to you than ever.

· Tantrums assist your child's habits in the long run

In most cases, children release their emotions in different ways, like being aggressive, refusing to cooperate on simple duties, or having conflicts when sharing. These are common symptoms that your child is having emotional issues. Having tantrums will help the child purge the feelings that might affect his obedient and natural self.

· If the tantrums occur at home, they might not happen in public.

Whenever children want to express their emotions, they'll often choose to get upset at home where they believe parents are there to listen. Forcing your children to keep it together in public and at home will make tension exacerbate. So, try to find space and time to pay attention to your child's upset feelings within the house. This will reduce the bottled-up feelings they'll carry to other destination.

· The child is doing things that many people don't remember how to do.

While the child grows and matures, one's crying tends to reduce. Partially this is due to maturing and learning to control one's emotions. Partly, it's based on learning to be part of the society that doesn't accept emotional expression. When parents get stressed and angry with their children, it's often because the adults want a good cry as well. It's difficult for grown people, especially men, to gain a sense of connection and safety to express their feelings. Therefore, allow your child to have the mood-improving tantrum to encourage their emotions to flow freely.

· Tantrums can be healing for the parent.

When you're there for your toddler's tantrums, it triggers immense feelings in you. When you were a child, your parents might not have paid attention to your outburst with sympathy. Your toddler's upset outbursts can activate memories of how your parents used to treat you, which you might not be conscious of recalling. Parenting can help you heal your emotional hardships when you gain support and an opportunity to listen to yourself.

Chapter 7: Into The World Of A Young Teenager

Surpassing the stage of young child development is no easy task. It is the most crucial and vital stage of disciplining because it is considered to be the peak of the child's developmental years. Raising and training them well in this stage will surely help the parents in the next mountain to cross which is their teenage years.

From the age of 13 to 19, your kid is considered an adolescent. This stage of growth is the toughest and hardest time to discipline your child. This is the time where they start to know more things about the world and with that comes a load of questions and inquiries. This is when they start to reason with you, talk back to you and insist upon their own will. This is also the time where they want to be most independent and bossing them around will more likely make them want to rebel against you.

A typical parent will usually start looking ahead to the adolescent river they are about to pass when their child turns the age of 13. They almost always expect an encounter of negative situations that will give way to a ton of consequences that will cost them their child's future. There is peer pressure, vices such as drinking and smoking, drug abuse, premarital sex, teenage pregnancy and many more. Teaching them the right kind of discipline in situations like these even became a much harder task as supposed to making them do their household chores.

Peer pressure springs out from the actions and demands of the friends surrounding your child. At this age, your kid sharpens his or her social skills by making new friends and interacting with them at school. As a parent, the first thing you need to teach your child is to choose his or her friends wisely. He or she must surround his or herself with peers that are responsible, disciplined and are good influences. Starting with a good group will surely help your kid broaden his or her connections with the right kind of people as he or she grows up.

Another thing you, as a parent, can do is to always keep your child on your team. It is important to remind your children that no matter what, family comes first. It is okay to highlight the importance of friendship among peers. However, make sure that your child will put your family first above anyone or anything else. This includes listening and putting more value to your advices and instructions as compared to that of your kid's friends.

Usually, vices among teenagers spring out from peer pressure among their acquaintances and to some extent, even in their own circle of friends. This includes drinking, smoking partying, doing drugs and more. Though this problem might come a bit later in their mid-teenage years, it is best to properly talk to them about it earlier rather than you catching them in the act of doing these vices already.

Instead of just saying no to all of these vices, explain thoroughly the reason behind such hindrances to these. This will help your children understand why it is prohibited than merely not doing it because you said so. Do not forget to mention the consequences and negative effects of drinking, smoking and drugs because this can be a good trick into scaring your children to avoid such vices.

After lecturing your child about this, expect yourself to put trust in them to actually decide for themselves. You did your part. You should let them do theirs. Some teenagers usually do vices because their parents accuse them of doing it even if they are actually not. Do not speculate and come up with conclusions right away. Trust your children that they can say 'no' for themselves.

However, some teenagers are usually gullible and easily manipulated by their friends. These are the type of people who easily falls into the trap of peer pressure. As a parent, you need to anticipate problems in the case your child can't say 'no' for themselves. In the event that you catch them doing such vices, be firm and strict in saying 'no' for them. This will then test how well you have disciplined your child because if they instilled enough respect for you as their parent, they would follow your command and stop their vices.

A good parent also talks to his or her child. A lot of teenagers develop vices because of certain problems and difficulties they are facing in their life. They make use of the vice as an escape from the pained reality that they have. Do not assume that you know every single thing that your child is going through. There are those kids that awfully stay silent of their problems. Do not be afraid to ask your child because that is what good parents do.

The next big thing your teenager faces is dating. Whether you like it or not, your child will go through this stage at this certain age. He or she will have his or her first crush, first date, first kiss and many other romantic firsts. This is normal, this is part of growing up. The more you accept it, the easier it is for you to communicate with your child about it.

When your teenager shows signs of infatuation over someone, it is the best time to start 'the talk.' Again, do not be afraid to ask and know your child's date. It is better to be informed rather than knowing nothing about the person your child is interacting with. However, a good parent knows how to set limits and boundaries regarding this because first and foremost you are a parent and your responsibility is to keep your child safe, physically and emotionally.

You have to set your rules regarding dating. It is important that you make them strict but at the same time, reasonable enough that your child will not insist of rebelling against them. You do not want that to happen. Along with the rules is the proper implementation of it. If you say curfew is 10 o'clock, the curfew is 10 o'clock. Impose consequences for the rules they break in order for them to exercise responsibility, even in dating.

When your child reaches a certain age of maturity, let's say around the age of 15 to 18, it is also your responsibility to teach them about sex. Do not rely on basic sex education lectures that the school provides. Devote a talk regarding this subject because your child needs to hear this from you. They might have questions about the subject that they can only ask from people who they feel comfortable with, and teachers are not one of them. Instead of asking it from their peers who might give them the wrong information, it is best that they ask and hear of it from you.

Helping your child say no to premarital sex is not an easy task. However, you can use these 3 arguments from spiritual, emotional and physical perspectives in order to help you explain to your child why sex is worth the wait.

For the spiritual aspect, abstaining from premarital sex protects your child from God's judgement. If you raised your child in a Christian environment, surely he or she fears the Lord. And the bible says (Hebrews 13:4) "marriage should be honored by all, and the marriage bed kept pure, for God will judge the adulterer and all the sexually immoral." Between heaven and hell, you can surely convince your child that saying no to sex means a thousand lifetimes in heaven.

For the emotional aspect, saying 'no' to premarital sex protects your child from suspicion and provides trust. You have to explain to your child that when they grow up and experience marriage, the key factor to a successful one is trust. Now, building trust between couples require a lot of sacrifices. This includes waiting to have sex until after marriage. This will truly strengthen their trust factor and will avoid suspicions and jealousy within themselves. Thus, by abstaining from sex, your child is actually building up a great foundation for his or her marriage in the future. And as a parent, you need to emphasize that even if the results of their actions will be reflected in the far future, it will always be worth it.

For the physical aspect, refraining from premarital sex protects your child from fear and provides peace of mind. Premarital sex paves the way to a lot of sexually transmitted diseases, both curable and incurable. Also, it leads to teenage pregnancy. By merely abstaining from it, it saves your kid the trouble of constantly thinking about whether or not she is pregnant, whether or not he or she is safe. There are a lot of consequences when the physical product of premarital sex occurs to your child.

Being a parent is no easy task, especially when your child reaches his or her adolescent years. There are more temptations and complications that you, as a parent, should always address properly. You have to constantly educate your child about it because that is what good parents do. Do not leave everything up for your child to learn because it is always better to teach them something right and factual than risking their learnings to something that might have been wrong and biased.

Chapter 8: Feelings Of Dyslexic Child

Anger

Emotional Problems brought by dyslexia occur because of the frustration that surrounds the dyslexic. This frustration creates produces anger. Dyslexic children often vent their anger to their parents. The reason behind this is because they trust their parents very well. However, this action may be quite critical to the parents who desperately tried to help their child.

As the child reach adolescence, wherein the society expects him to be independent, he uses his anger to break away to those people on which he feels so dependent. Due to these factors, the parent will have difficulty in helping their teenage child. Per tutoring can be a big help to him.

Anxiety

Anxiety is one of the most common emotional problems of dyslexic child. They became worried and fearful due to the frustration in their school. These feelings are brought about dyslexia. Failure becomes extremely anxiety provoking.

This anxiety makes the child to avoid things that frightens him. Some teachers and parents misinterpret this anxiety. But the fact is that, this is not apathy but more on emotional problem and anxiety.

Depression

Common complexity of dyslexia. Even though children in this condition is not depressed, they tend to have a higher attachment for intense feeling of heartaches. Most dyslexic child has low confidence. They are worried to show their anger to their environment that's why they tend to

turn it on themselves making them feel pained and broken. A depressed child is unable to show that he feels sad. He becomes more aggressive and behaves to show off these painful things.

Self-image

The child who has dyslexia has vulnerable self-image which is caused by anxiety and frustration.

Once the children encountered failure, they feel inferiority. Instead of being powerful and efficient they feel that the environment take control on their action. They feel so powerless and incompetent than others. While other sees that failure is a motivation to try and work harder for dyslexic failures means that he is stupid.

They tend to be ashamed and loss their self-esteem.

Family Relationship Problems

Dyslexia leaves a very big impact to family. This is often overlooked because of its effect.

One of the most common effects of it to the family is the sibling's rivalry. Other children got jealous because most of the time, money and attention of their parents are given to the dyslexic. They used this reason to rebel. But the dyslexic doesn't ask for this attention for he sees himself weak. The parents should give out reasons to the dyslexic child for him to fully understand his condition and to help him face his failures and emotions.

How Can Teachers and Parents Help Dyslexic Child?

Early interventions will provides greatest chance of success to dyslexic child. Here are some tips for parents and teachers in handling their child.

Observe and evaluate the child's need and necessities.

Give them the assessment of special learning that they need in class.

Always consider the academic and behavioral needs through formal and informal diagnostic observation.

Select and use the proper instructional practices. Determine which is the best practice that will suit to the child's learning skills.

Consider the age in choosing learning strategies and make sure to gain the cooperation of the child.

Combine different strategies to provide the child best assessment.

Identify the materials needed for the child to learn better.

Tell the children about alternative resources that they may use in solving homework.

Here are the different steategies that the teacher performed while conducting an academic lesson:

Use different visual and audio presentations. This will help the child to be more attentive and focus. They can easily learn the lesson because of these aids.

Observed the child's performance. You have to check the student's performance to know if they are able to commit and learn. You can ask them individually or you can make seat work for them to solve.

Evaluate student. Know the student who needs more assistance and has learning difficulty. Watch over about their comprehension and skills.

*Control the Noise Level - you should monitor the noise level in your classroom and provide the correct feedback for the children. Remind the child about your behaviors expectations.

Dyslexic Children often have difficulty in focusing. Teachers can help them through these transitions:

Create and Provide advance warnings.

Check the child's assignments.

Preview the next lesson.

INSTRUCTIONAL PRACTICES

BEHAVIOR MANAGEMENT

- These are the strategies that teachers do to help their child learn effective self control:

PRAISING THE CHILD

- Praises will encourage the child to act more appropriately. It will help them to be motivated and develop self esteem.

REPRIMANDS

- Tell the child what's wrong with his behavior. Never put it directly on the child but rather on his attitude.

GENERAL PRINCIPLES

Effective mentors should help their child in learning the lessons that they introduce to them. Taking principles of effective teaching and instruction will provide an effective learning skill and productive environment to the child.

In beginning lessons, here are some strategies that the teacher may do:

- Recap and reviews the previous lessons.

- Remind the child about the information stated on the previous lessons.

- Settle and review problems before proceeding to the next lesson and learning expectations.

- Tell the students what are the things to be expected from the lessons.

- Remind your child about behavioral expectations.

- Show enthusiasm and interest in learning.

- Use technology to make the learning strategy to be more efficient.

- Make a way to simplify complex lessons.

☐ Prepare a report on child's achievement and behavior.

Chapter 9: Understand The Differences Between Motherhood And Fatherhood

Make no mistake. Fathers are not second mothers. Every parent has their own role in their child's development, which is different from the other parent's approaches. Of course, biology and human nature will influence a parent's behavior, but gender ideologies, social values and the parents' culture will also play a role. Whether you are a mum or dad, the way you communicate with your child will be different from your counterpart's approach.

Mothers usually use tender words that they feel are appropriate for a child age level, even when they have grown into full blown adults. On the other hand, unless a child is an infant, the father will not adjust his language when talking to a child. However, while both mothers and fathers are undoubtedly different, both of you can make a great team if you want.

Mothers tend to be more repetitive with their children as opposed to dads, while fathers speak less often to their children. As such, the mother plays a major role in prompting the development of vocabulary and linguistic skills. On the other hand, dads tend to interact more on a physical level, engaging in tactile and physical games with their children. Some of these activities include playing with the child on the playground, rough and tumble and tickling games. These are helpful in encouraging fine motor and visual development. On their part, mothers are more likely to engage their children in non-tactile and predictable games such as peek a boo. These generally involve the use of toys and more talking and are important to enhance a child's cognitive and social development.

A mother's disciplinary action normally involves emphasis on sympathy, care and helpfulness. This kind of discipline is more helpful and teaches the child about rules. On the other hand, when a father disciplines their child, he is more likely to emphasis justice, fairness, duty and the consequences of actions. Men tend to be strict and systematic when reinforcing the rules that the children are supposed to follow. As Such, both parenting styles supplement each other.

Mothers are more likely to be predictable than their counterpart fathers. The way a mother picks up a child and holds them is usually the same, ninety percent of the time, despite the circumstances. On the other hand, the way that a father picks up a child and holds them will vary with the reason for picking the kid. For instance, when playing, the father may pick the child up by his/her feet, and under the arms when consoling them.

Age Level Discipline Approaches

Generally, a father's approach to discipline is usually quite different from a mother's approach. You see it everywhere. Daddy tosses little Junior up in the air. As he flies up, squealing giggles are heard as the mom pleads, "Be careful, not so high!" This is because dads and moms have a different point of view when it comes to parenting, like nearly anything else in life. Fathers offer rules, challenges and adventure, while mothers offer hope, empathy and security. These discrepancies also come into play when it comes to disciplining the little ones. However, it is important to note early that no one approach is better than the next. Rather, it is when you blend both of these approaches that they can become as effective.

*A Fathers' love

A mother's emotional bond with her child is a natural one. This is hugely due to the fact that she spends nine months nurturing the baby inside her womb, worked effortlessly to bring the infant into the world, and took care of his/her every need as a baby. You will find that by the age of 8 weeks, the baby already knows who to turn to for dependable security and comfort. However, the interaction between a father and his child is very different. In most cases, the father usually spends the most part of the early months of the child's development outside the happy circle created by the mother and child. As such, the father has to earn his position in the relationship through such efforts as touch, interactions and talk that will build the child's trust.

*A Mothers' love

Women tend to be interested more in people. You will not often find them chatting about golf trophies and job performance or the weekend basketball scores over cups of coffee. They will most likely be talking about who is getting married, who is in love, or who has been hurt and what they can do to help. Therefore, when it comes to discipline, moms approach the situation with an interest in social and emotional well being. They strive to find a connection between them and the little ones, as well as to emphasize hopefulness and goodness. For example, if a mother catches her little child wrestling with another child over a toy, she is more likely to point out the impact of the argument on both children and how both of them can be happier if they played nicely.

*Fathers stress on performance

You will rarely find men sitting around a table chatting over bottles of beer about their emotions. Often, they talk about adventures and experiences such as fishing trips and camping, or interests such as woodcarving and football. Fathers are very simple. It is either you follow the rules or suffer the consequences. In most cases, they will not spend time elaborating reasons and feelings and the importance of maintaining healthy relationships when they find their children fighting over toys. Rather, their initial reaction is to storm in and order the children to stop the behavior or else...

*Bring them together

One problem that comes to view when one side of disciplining takes too much precedence is unhealthy development. Providing your child with too much of the loving, and safety conscious type of parenting can make your child feel too much smothered and even fear to try new things. On the other hand, too much of the authoritarian type of parenting from the father's side can make your child feel judged and feel a lack of comfort or unconditional love and approval. If you want to make both these divergent techniques work, you will have to combine them to give your child a steady foundation. The child will grow up with a drive, understanding, firmness, sympathy, structure and love. When both mothers and fathers find a way to work together, they can provide an interweaving of complementary techniques that work perfectly together, mainly because of their differences.

One of the most common setbacks in raising a family for most parents is the right approach to discipline. How do you keep your toddler away from the DVD player? What discipline approach should you take when your preschooler wrongfully gets into a fight? How do you make your teenage daughter respect your authority? No matter the age, it is crucial that you stay consistent as long as discipline is concerned. If you as parents don't stick to the rules, consequences and punishments you set up, do not expect your kids to either. Here are some expert ideas to help you out:

Ages 0 to 2

Since babies of this age are naturally curious, the best approach is to eliminate any temptations such as video and TV equipment, jewelry, stereos, and cleaning supplies as well as any medication out of their reach. If you find your toddler crawling to a perceived dangerous item, just affirm them "NO" and quickly remove the child from the area or find something else to distract him/her with. Timeouts can work perfectly with toddlers in terms of discipline. For example, if you find your child throwing food, biting or hitting, you should explain why the behavior is unacceptable and then direct them to a designated timeout location. This could be a bottom stair or a kitchen chair, just for a minute or two to calm things down. Toddlers do not work well with longer timeouts. On the other hand, be sure not to slap, hit or spank your child, no matter the age. Toddlers are less likely to make a connection between their actions and physical punishment. Rather, they will only feel the impact of the hit. Also, keep in mind that kids learn from their parents' behaviors. Therefore, be sure to present a role model material in your behavior. For example, it will make more sense if you do not have cluttered items in your room when screaming orders to your child to pick up his scattered toys on the floor.

Ages 3 to 5

At this age, your child has grown and is beginning to understand the connection between deeds and consequences. Take advantage of this and communicate the rules of your home. Emphasis your expectations from them before you implement punishment for a certain behavior. For example, if you find your child has decorated the living room with crayons, discuss politely with them why this kind of behavior is unacceptable and the consequences for repeating the action a second time. You could tell them they will have to help clean the wall and they will not be allowed to use the crayons for the whole day. If the child repeats the same mistake after a couple of days, remind them that crayons are for paper and then reinforce the set consequences. The earlier you set consequences for misbehaviors in your home, the better. While it is common for some parents to be lenient on certain misbehavior or not follow through on some set consequences or punishment, this is setting a bad precedent.

The key to effective discipline is consistency, and it is vital for you as parents to decide together what the rules are and then abide by them. On the other hand, do not forget to reward good behavior. Some parents tend to underestimate the power of even a single of praise to their children. Realize that discipline is not only about punishment and rules; it is also about acknowledging good behavior. For example, it is more effective to tell your child that you are proud of him/her for sharing their toys at a playgroup, rather than punishing them for doing the opposite – not sharing. In addition, be specific when giving out the praise, rather than just telling the child, "Good Job".

If you find that your child continues to exhibit unacceptable behavior continuously despite your efforts, you could come up with a chart that has a box for each day of the week. You can then decide after how long your child can misbehave before you punish them, or in that case, after how long they must display proper behavior before they are rewarded. Post it on the fridge and then monitor the good and bad behaviors of the day. This will give you and your child a concrete view of how it is going. If this works in your favor, do not forget to complement the child for learning to control their behavior and for overcoming any stubborn obstacle. You should issue rewards and consequences on a daily basis. Long term consequences tend to have little impact.

Kids at this age group also work well with timeouts. Find a suitable timeout area that is free of any distractions and that will force your child to think about his/her bad behavior. Remember that sending your child to his/her room will have no impact if they have video games, TV or a computer in there. Remember to implement the timeout according to the age of the child. Experts recommend that the best approach is to set one minute for each year of age. However, telling your kids what the right thing to do is equally as important (or more) than just telling them what the wrong thing is. For instance, rather than just telling them not to jump on the couch, you could tell them to sit on the furniture and put their feet on the floor.

Ages 6 to 8

This age group also works well with consequences and timeouts. Again, the key is consistency. Make sure you implement your promises of discipline or else you will risk undermining your own authority. Let your kids believe that you mean what you say. While this does not necessarily mean being a dictator and not allowing for small margins of error, you should ensure that you act on what you say. However, make sure that you do not make unrealistic consequences or actions for certain misbehaviors. For example, telling your kid not to slam the door or else he/she will never watch television again in anger is simply hard to follow through and will only weaken your threats. On the other hand, if on the way to the beach you notice some squabbling in the backseat of the car, be sure to turn the car around if it does not stop. You will find the gained credibility with your kids much more precious than a lost day at the beach. On the other, make sure you do not implement huge punishments as these tend to withdraw your parental powers. For example, grounding your son or daughter for one month may make them feel less motivated to change their behavior since everything has already been taken away.

Ages 9 to 12

You can discipline your child at this age group with natural consequences, just like with a child of any age. Children at this age group are maturing and tend to bid for more responsibility and independence. Therefore, the most appropriate and effective strategy to apply at this time is to teach them how to deal with the consequences of their actions. For example, if your son fails to finish their homework before bedtime, he or she should stay up doing it.

Like with kids of any other age group, these kids work well with natural consequences. Kids at this age group are maturing, and so tend to request more responsibility and independence. Therefore, the best approach is to teach them how to deal with the consequences of their actions. For example, if your son fails to finish his homework before bedtime, should you lend him a hand or make him stay up doing it? Probably not. Doing this will see you lose the opportunity to teach him an important lesson in life. If he goes to school without his homework, he will eventually suffer bad grade. While it is natural for you to want to rescue your child from their mistakes, sometimes letting them fail will do them a favor in the long run. Kids at this age will see the consequences of behaving inappropriately and will therefore avoid making the same mistakes. However, if you find that the natural consequences are not helping much, you could set your own to help change the behavior.

Ages 13 and above

By now, chances are you have already set the foundation and your child knows what is expected of them and that you are credible when it comes to rules and consequences. This is not the time to let your guard down. Your teenager needs discipline just as much as younger kids. Just like with the previous age groups, you need to set a bedtime and follow through, and also set boundaries. Establish rules regarding dating, curfews, visits by friends, and homework. Discuss these rules with your teenager as early as possible to avoid any misunderstandings. While your teenager is bound to rebel from time to time, they will also realize that you are in control. Most people do not know this, but teenagers also need you to set limits and restore order in their lives, even with all the freedom and responsibility granted to them. When your teen breaks a rule, the best plan of action would be to take away a privilege. While it is okay to withdraw their car, for example, for a week, be sure to discuss with them why coming home way past the set curfew is worrisome and unacceptable. However, be sure to also give him/her some control over certain things. This will go along way in reducing the power struggles you encounter and make your teenager respect the decisions that you have to make. Some of the decisions you could let your teen handle could be about hairstyles, school clothes, or even their room's condition. As your teenager gets older, you could extend the realm of their control to include irregular relaxed curfews. It is also important to focus on the positive things. You could let your teenager earn a later curfew if he/she demonstrates positive behavior as opposed to setting an earlier curfew for punishment for irresponsible behavior.

A note on spanking

The issue of spanking has been controversial since time immemorial. Here are some of the reasons why experts do not encourage spanking:

*It teaches that it is alright to hit others when you are angry

*It can physically harm children

*It makes them fear their parents instead of teaching them good behavior

Chapter 10: Foundation Of Parenting

If this is your first child, chances are that you are not sure exactly how to parent your toddler. While everyone parents differently, there are a few things that should stay the same across the board. Some of them are seen as controversial topics, when in reality they are not. There are just some parents out there who are, for some reason, against certain things.

This chapter gives you some ideas of the expectations of parenthood. If you do not agree with one of the points in this chapter, that is perfectly fine! You should parent as you see fit. This is just a rundown of some of the more common things because there are so many contradictory articles out there about how to raise your child.

Emotional Support

This is something that nowadays is not super controversial like it used to be. In the older days, there were parents who thought that being there emotionally for your child 24/7 was too much and that you were spoiling your child. There were parents who thought children should not get upset when they were being yelled at and that they had no right to be angry. The truth is, toddlers experience emotions at a higher rate than we do, and there are a lot of parents that act as if they have no right to have those emotions when, in reality, they do.

You should always teach your child that is okay to show emotion as long as they do it respectfully. Such as, it is okay to be angry; however, it is not okay to be disrespectful or to yell and scream. Likewise, if you are going to teach them that yelling is not the way to express anger, then you should not yell at your child when you are angry. Children learn more from what they see and less from what they hear, so you truly have to be careful when you are trying to teach them new things.

Teach your children about emotions. The movie Inside Out is a great foundation for teaching children about emotions and how to handle them. It is also great for toddlers because it is animated and colorful, so it should catch their attention. After you watch the movie, go over what you learned, and if your toddler gets hooked on it, at least it has some educational value to it.

Be there for your child emotionally. Listen to them when they are trying to communicate with you, and be there to help the get what they need. As they grow, it will be a great foundation for teaching them how to handle and sort through their own emotions.

Helicopter Parenting Is a Big NO

Yes, you read that correctly. The new trend of being a helicopter parent is actually detrimental to the development of your toddler. You want to control everything they do and everything they learn so that you can ensure that they are only learning what you want them to and that they are not learning anything bad. However, your toddler will not learn on your schedule, and trying to force them to do so will cause them to miss out on learning something valuable elsewhere. Your toddler needs freedom to explore.

They need to be able to play with books and play with toys. You can't force them to learn something if they are not ready to.

It is also detrimental to their ability to become self-sufficient. By doing everything for them and instructing them on every little detail in their lives, as they grow older, they will not be able to figure things out for themselves. Letting your child learn on their own at times will help them develop problem solving skills and some independence. Your child will one day be an adult, and being a helicopter parent will squash that ability.

Also, your toddler may be gearing up for preschool. This means they will be spending several hours a day without you. If you are a helicopter parent, this could lead to bad behavior in the classroom or an inability to make friends. You stunt your child's emotional and mental development by taking away the options of choice from your child. You want your toddler to be successful and to be smart, but forcing them to do it your way is not always the way to go.

Introducing Learning

This is something that is very controversial. Of course you do not want to be a helicopter parent, but you want to make sure that you are giving your child the foundation he or she needs before starting school. Some parents say that when children are toddlers, it is a time to play and enjoy being a child. While it is true that they learn through play, it is also true that right now their brains are developing at a rapid pace, and it is the potential time for learning.

No one ever said that the two couldn't be combined. Teaching kids through various play activities is a great way to teach them new things. This will be talked about more in a different chapter that is all about learning through play and different activities that you can do with your toddler.

It is important to introduce some subjects to toddlers to get them on the right track for life, but the most important thing they should learn is how to connect with others. Teaching your child to play nicely and to make friends is one of the most valuable learning experiences out there.

How to Handle the Stove and Other Dangers

Toddlers seem drawn to danger. The reason is unknown, but it could be an innate wonder of things that seem to scream don't touch. Children want to know why they shouldn't touch. They want to know why something is bad for them. It is all part of learning and the developing brain. You do not want them to get hurt, but they don't seem to understand the dangers. Scare tactics are seen as cruel, but there are a few tips to teaching your toddler the dangers of the stove and other things that might hurt them. The biggest one is the stove because you can put chemicals up out of a toddler's reach, so we will start with the stove.

Let's face it. Eventually a baby gate is not going to keep your toddler out of the kitchen. Plus there are many valuable things that they can learn by being allowed to help you in the kitchen, such as doing dishes or helping prepare dinner. However, the kitchen is a dangerous place, and the number one danger is the stove. Third-degree burns are a real possibility with stoves. How do you keep your kid away from the stove without them getting hurt?

Explain the dangers of heat to your kid. Show them a few mild pictures of burns. (First degree works the best because it is usually just redness. Sunburn would even work in this case.) Tell them that is what can happen if they touch a hot stove. This will get the point across without them having to learn the hard way. If they understand just how much they can get hurt, they will generally not want to go near a stove.

There are also sharp objects that you have to be careful with. Children want to help their parents with everything in the kitchen, but when it comes to chopping things, you may be afraid to let them do so. There are kid friendly knives out there, but they are recommended for children 5 years and older. So in the beginning, it is best to keep your toddler away from knives entirely. You can use the same tactic as with the stove, only with cuts. Show them a picture of something like a paper cut, or a very mild contusion. That way you do not freak them out, but you get your point to a level that your toddler can understand.

The hardest one is chemicals. How do you get your toddler to understand that chemicals are dangerous? Put all of your chemicals in a certain area. Explain to your toddler that anything that comes from that area is for parental use only. Tell them that it can make them very sick, so they should stay away from it. Children don't like being sick. Use a time they were sick as an example of what a chemical can do to them. The same with medicines.

Vaccinations

Okay, this is going to be one that not everyone agrees with; however, it is important that you have the right information to make decisions with. By now, you have probably made your choice on whether or not to vaccinate. Hopefully you have chosen to vaccinate. However, right now is when you can choose to turn down a few of those vaccinations. This section will go over the importance of vaccinations so that you understand just how essential vaccinations can be to a healthy child.

Many parents are scared that vaccines cause autism. This is not true, and you may wonder where these parents priority lie. Yes, autism can be a struggle to deal with, but the diseases that these vaccines prevent are way worse. They can cause a painful and horrible death, or even life-long physiological problems if survived. Vaccinations keep children from suffering these once common diseases. However, there is no worry, because the doctor who came up with that theory was proved to have falsified his information, and he was stripped of his license. Dr. Andrew Wakefield presumably made the entire thing up because he was losing money on funding. No one could recreate the results, and further investigation showed he put children who were already diagnosed with autism through a lot of painful procedures to try to prove his theory. You can read more about him here at:

So what is the correlation between the MMR vaccine and autism? Well, the only thing that makes it seem possible at all is that the MMR vaccine is given between 18 months and 2 years. This is the time when autism is generally diagnosed in children; however, the truth is, children with autism are born with it. There is no reason to fear vaccines for the reason that most do.

Some people are skeptical about all of the new vaccines that are out. The only reason there are so many new vaccines in this generation is due to the amazing advances in technology and medicine. This has allowed more vaccinations to be created for viruses such as meningitis and mono. There are also more sessions of a vaccine so that your immune system does not have to take a big hit at once, but is still protected. There are no new vaccines out just to steal money, in fact most child vaccines can be acquired for free at a local health department.

The bottom line is that vaccines are important. When you vaccinate your child, you are protecting them from an illness that could end their life. You are also preventing your child from being a carrier of the disease, so you are also protecting a child who can't be vaccinated due to health reasons. So in reality, you are protecting not one, but many children by choosing to vaccinate completely.

Getting a Pet

Your child is at an age now, where they can start taking on more responsibility. This means that many parents are considering getting their child a pet. This can be a great idea, if you as a parent are prepared to take on the responsibility. A toddler is not capable of walking a dog and cleaning up after it on a regular basis. Nor is a toddler capable of remembering to feed and water an animal all the time.

However, there are some perks to getting a family pet while your child is a toddler. You should always refer to the pet as a family pet so that everyone has to share the responsibility and you are not putting it all on your child for reasons we will discuss here shortly.

A pet growing up helps teach a toddler compassion, along with it being the start of a good lesson of responsibility. Your toddler cannot be completely responsible for the animal, but getting them into a routine of taking care of the animal will help them understand that there are some things that have to be done every day. This is a good way to teach children to love those who depend on you as well. There are a lot of life lessons that can be taught by getting a pet.

However, as stated above, you have to be committed to keeping the pet until its life has come to an end. It is really hard on children to lose a pet because their parents got tired of caring for the animal day in and day out. This usually stems from calling the pet the child's pet, rather than the family pet. This puts the pressure on the child to take care of the animal, and toddlers just are not ready for that level of responsibility.

No matter what you choose for your child, the best thing to keep in mind is that you want to do what is in their best interest. You may find that you have to adjust some of the things that you found important along this journey. Whether it be how you discipline or things that you find punishable. Children will make you wonder how you ever survived before them.

Explore Different Interests

Every parent has an idea of what they want their child to be when they grow up. However, you cannot force your desires on your child. You may hear of the man who wants his son to be a football star, and the son later finds out that he wants to be an artist, and the father gets angry. This is not a good way to raise your child. You can start young with encouraging them to explore different interests.

Having a kid that has well-rounded interests will help them well into the future and will make it easier for them to make friends as they can relate to different types of people. You want to encourage your child to be fun loving and to enjoy different things. A child can like both sports and art. That is perfectly okay. It will look good on future college applications as well. However, you have many years before you start worrying about college.

A good foundation for a well-rounded child starts at a young age. Be active in their life. Play games with your child. Take them to the zoo, not only to look at the animals but also to learn about them. Guided tours for zoos are extremely helpful, and your child will enjoy seeing all the different animals. Get a ball and play catch, no matter if your child is a boy or a girl. Teach your child how to climb. Join a parent and child painting class.

The important thing is that you get your child involved in the world around them. Show them that there is so much more to the world than the toys that they have at home. Teach them to enjoy more than video games and the television. Even if you are a busy parent, make time to show your kid the world, or make sure that they are in the care of a daycare or babysitter that will help you with that.

Childcare

Most parents today are either single-parent families or two-parent families with both parents working. You have to be prepared with childcare, and you probably have already lined up a family member or daycare to watch your child. The question is, is your child in the right environment that really stimulates learning development? The truth is that you are entrusting your child to a provider of childcare for about as many hours a day as they would be going to school. If your child is just left to do whatever or sat in front of the television, they are not getting any mental stimulation. You want to find someone or someplace that provides preschool or kindergarten prep.

Remember, toddlers are sponges, and the more that you expose them to learning materials, the more they will learn. You want them to have the best foundation that is possible, and that often means switching childcare providers if your child is not getting the mental stimulation they need.

Raising a child can be hard work. Remember, these are just some suggestions on things to think about when you hit the toddler stage. You want to do what is best for your family and your child, and some things in this list may not be feasible for you. However, if you wish to use these, by all means do.

Chapter 11: If It Doesn't Work, Change It

I met 8 year-old Brain as a boy who was always out of control (According to the mother's description). He was attending anger issue classes. The situation was simple. Brian's mother had lost control of him and Brian was winning, loving every minute he spent with his mother. But Brian wouldn't dare to act like this in the presence of his Dad.

This popular condition causes big trouble in the marriage than it causes in the parent to child relationship. What is going on here is that the child views the father differently from the mother.

Little Brian got his mother running round the house. So much that she has forgotten that she was the adult here. Getting Brian to school was war. She would run after the little child round the house yelling and chasing after him. But if Dad was around, Brian becomes an angel. Do you know what is going on? I am sure you do. Brian is in charge and the mother is not.

I started with the mother. I was able to understand that the Mother does much of the parenting while Dad was at work. The father was fed up with his wife because she couldn't control Brian so the child has placed both parent in a crisis.

One parent represented fear while the other represented fun. The Dad would have to just stare at him and he would be in his best behavior but the mother on the other hand would have to scream and chase Brian round the house just to get him to behave. Like most mums, she would try to sit Brian down and talk some senses into him. But this technique keeps failing. You can't talk to a young child using adult language. They don't get it, they are children. She did this all the time and she got the same result. If it doesn't work, change it!

Please note that fear is a greater motivator to children than pain. Brian's Dad produced fear while the Mother gave out pain. Screaming, chasing and smacking was just a short term pain for little Brian. This process trained Brian to look for no other attention than that relating to pain. Smacks and screams became a normal thing to him. The mother needed to change her way of thought. Try something different. Giving Brian the Adult talk all the time wasn't helping why should she continue?

You should never allow your child to be disrespectful. When I meet with parents who have children like Brian, I ask them one question; did you act like this to your parents at that age? What I get is a big No. Most of the time like Brian when he sees his Dad, these parents are TOO AFRAID to do wrong. Then why do you allow your child to continue like that? The response I get is always disappointing. It shows that the parents are in a stage of helplessness. "I don't know why, I don't just know why"

The true answer should be; I am afraid. Parents like Brian's mother are afraid of themselves as parents. Does this sound ridiculous to you? A parent afraid of parenting. An adult scared of her child. The parents become scared that they believe in their mind that it is better or easier for them to let the child misbehave than for them to confront it.

A child needs your love, we know but most importantly he/she needs your training. Train that child, don't fold your hands and watch things go bad.

I once met two parents of a wild 15 year old in tears. Jane was just like Brian. But she was out of control of both parents. Obviously, she must have received that bad parenting technique when she was around Brian's age. They listed what they have been able to do, I was surprised:

They took away her mobile phone

Grounded her for weeks. Meaning no going out except school

Stopped her from the internet and computer.

That was all. Father and Mother were literarily in tears. After taking the three regular steps and nothing seems to work. I just had to give it to them raw because I felt their pain. I introduced them to the no privacy technique. This technique may sound extreme. The parents are to remove Jane's bedroom door, remove all her clothes, trinkets and other furniture. They are to empty the room totally until what is left is the mattress on the floor and the school uniform. As I was explaining all these, I could read the terror in the eyes of the parent. I didn't mind. I also told the parents to ring all friends of Jane and parents. And tell them not to allow Jane into their house under no circumstance.

The mother was getting uncomfortable. I was expecting that. Finally she voiced out and said that they couldn't do it. And the father didn't surprise me either. Aren't we taking this too far? He asked.

Yes, I was expecting this and I went into action. I began to shout at them. This technique wasn't to correct the child but the parents. I remember saying something like: How come you two are telling me that you can't do this? Are you bad parents or good ones? Why do you keep hiding behind your own poor attitude?

What I was trying to do was simple. I was trying to create that extreme fear and panic and it was working. Humans make up thoughts and emotions that result in behavior. These parents have created that state of chaos and fear around Jane's parenting process.

I watched them as they begin to make excuses for their daughter. According to them, I was taking the punishment too far. They called it punishment already! Three of us were in the middle of a heated debate as I have successfully placed both parents in that state of fear and dread. I even threatened them saying that I would report to the authorities that they were bad parents.

Face pale, breathing intense looking almost like a panic attack. This was the transformation point. Instinctively, the mother continued to place her hand on her chest and the father's tummy kept moving in and out also. Signs of anxiety. I told them to sit on a special chair and I told the mother to close her eyes, imagine that fear shrink to size of a postage stamps. After few minutes both parents were fearless. You cannot cure a phobia of spiders unless you face spiders. This is why I needed these parents to face and experience pain. You can't help someone overcome fear of heights if he fails to climb high.

That session was the life-changing session for them. I explained further and the next time they visited I could see the broad smile on their faces. They told me that Jane had screamed loudly, thrown things around the house and did run away to the comfort of her best friend's house. And just as the parents have requested, she wasn't welcomed into the house of her best friend.

We really need to note here that sometimes there is always someone, a female especially who would always want to be a mother Teresa for the child. They are mostly single mothers looking for attention and love. There is nothing bad there but you should make your intentions known perfectly. The parents took to every detail given to them. Doors locked like a fortress and lights turned off. The parents were panicking but they knew all would be alright. Please understand that this was a girl who had roamed the streets for two years, drinks, smokes, and put all sort of fear into her parents.

1:30am in the morning, they heard a knock on the door. It was Jane. I told them not to be quick to open but to listen to her voice. She was weeping, she had walked everywhere to seek shelter but couldn't find. The parents opened the door after they were much convinced that their daughter was truly in tears and was ready for the dos and don'ts the parents have drafted out. If she agreed she was to walk in, if not they would put off the lights and leave her to herself. It worked and to my surprise the father walked in the girl and she said something I would never forget. "Mum and Dad told me you put our family back together for us, thank you so much"

As a parent you shouldn't trick yourself into thinking that your child would do terrible things if you refuse to give them what they want. Children are expected to grow, they are required to test and understand emotions. Once you feel or you are afraid that your child would do something worse if you don't give her what she wants, you give in to that threat from him/her. You have just trained that child to mess with your feelings.

You shouldn't become a parent who is afraid to discipline his/her child. Yes, you want to make his childhood amazing, you want to offer her the best you can give but discipline comes first. It is wonderful to have a child who you love and you are ready to offer her the whole world but don't get fooled in that process. If discipline is not added to the early life of a child he or she would grow up to be a chaos to the society. If one method is not working, try another.

Chapter 12: A Positive Approach To Changing Children's Behaviors

Understanding the function of a child's behavior before deciding what to do about the behavior is a foundation of a positive behavior approach. When we understand the context in which the behavior we wish to change occurs, then we can change things in the context (rather than trying to change things in the child) to effectively change the behaviors.

A positive behavior approach goes beyond merely reacting to behaviors toward a far more proactive technique. This is especially effective with behaviors we wish to decrease or eliminate. Instead of only dealing with the consequences of an undesirable behavior, we can identify and modify what precedes this behavior to stop it before it occurs.

The story of the mother wanting her 20 minutes to cook described above is a good example. After determining that attention seemed to be the main function of the children's screaming and a lack of attention preceded the screaming, we developed a way for the mother to pay attention to the children before they began screaming, which eliminated the screaming. If you can identify what comes right before the behavior and change it, the behavior no longer occurs. Instead of figuring out ways to react to objectionable behaviors, we can figure out ways to modify the environment so that the behavior never occurs.

There are numerous illustrations of the effectiveness of this approach in the professional literature as well as in clinical practice. Among the more dramatic examples is the utility of positive strategies with self-injurious behaviors. Functional assessment of people who hurt themselves often shows that escape is the primary function. Teaching the person to request or otherwise signal the need for a break often dramatically reduces or eliminates these injurious behaviors. If you successfully address the function then you can prevent the behavior.

Another effective way to reduce unwanted behaviors is to concentrate on opposite behaviors, that is, think about and concentrate on what you want the child to do, not what you want the child to stop doing. Rather than making a fuss every time your child runs in the house, for example, you can instead make a fuss every time she walks. This not only shifts the focus away from undesirable behaviors to desired ones, but makes the competing behavior (walking) more attractive to the child. It seems to be a natural tendency to ignore desirable behaviors and attend to the undesirable ones, but training yourself to do the opposite will make you far more effective at changing behaviors. Focusing on desirable behaviors is not only more effective but far more pleasant, and your main goal of parenting should always be to enjoy your child.

Sticker Charts and Time-Out

Within 10 minutes of my first day on a new job as the psychologist in a preschool, I was assigned the case of Dan, a three year-old little boy who was hitting his classmates at least a dozen times a day. The teachers were putting Dan in time out every time he hit, the results of which suggesting this was not a terribly effective strategy.

Observation and a functional assessment suggested that the excited responses of distress Dan got from the teachers was his goal, suggesting power and control as the main function (attention appeared to be a secondary function). The goal of intervention was to use this information to get Dan to stop hitting. Being an advocate of positive behavioral strategies, I needed to address the function while shifting the focus away from the hitting and promoting the opposite behavior, which is not hitting.

What we came up with was a system that rewarded not hitting while having a consequence for hitting. This was accomplished with a sticker chart, a timer, and a box of special toys selected by Dan. The chart consisted of a five-box grid and stickers. The timer served to remind us to attend to Dan when he was not hitting. We'd set the timer for one minute, and when it went off, the teacher would look at Dan and praise whatever he was doing other than hitting ("Dan, I like the way you're playing with those cars") while moving a sticker into one of the boxes on the chart and then resetting the timer. When the final box got a sticker, then Dan got three minutes (timed with an hourglass egg timer) to play with his special toys. Whenever he hit someone, he was told, "No hitting" and a sticker was removed. Over time, the intervals increased to 30-45 minutes, and after about a week the hitting stopped.

The point is that we identified a specific behavior, addressed what we thought was the function, and shifted the focus to positive alternative behaviors. Time out can be effective at times but places the emphasis on reacting to problematic behaviors, which we wanted to avoid. Not only did Dan stop hitting, but after a couple of weeks he looked far more comfortable then he did when he was doing all that hitting. I think that he too liked the ability to achieve what he thought he needed to without resorting to problem behaviors.

This anecdote brings up another important point in behavior management, which is that children (and adults, for that matter) only do what they think will be worth their while. As most parents discover, "because we want them to" does not qualify as worth the child's while. Not only do we have to make it worth the child's while to do what it is we want them to do, but we need to tell them up front what is in it for them to do this behavior and to make it more attractive than the current situation. This is commonly known in Early Childhood as Grandma's Rule, i.e., "first you eat your peas, and then you get dessert", which is far more positive then "if you don't eat your peas, then you don't get dessert" as well as more effective. Dan stopped hitting because he gained much more by not hitting then from hitting, after which he learned how pleasant not hitting could be.

My favorite example occurred several years ago with my youngest child. My wife and I both work, and we would alternate taking Alexander to school. Whomever had school duty had to leave the house by 7:35 to avoid being late for work. We never made it out by 7:35.

After several months of complaining, threatening, begging, and general carrying on, I finally decided to think like a psychologist. My first question was, "What is Alexander's gain in being on time?" Making us happy certainly did not matter, we put on a great display every morning (power and control?), and there was no clear gain for getting ready on time.

Alexander's official bed time was 9:00 and he got in bed by 9:30, which made him think he was getting over on us and was an acceptable time for us. What I told him was that if he was ready by 7:35 or earlier, he got to stay up until 9:35; if we left the house after 7:35, then he went to bed at 9:00. I swear that we went from 0% success to 100% success in one day, and never again did we leave after 7:35.

Chapter 13: Self-Worth And Self-Awareness

Self-worth is described as optimistic self-imaging that should be instituted proactively by every individual; it does not usually occur inertly. People who expect peripheral factors to create a realistic and objective foundation for their self-worth will most likely be disappointed.

Self-confidence is the attitude that people hold about their optimistic view of themselves and their situations. Those who are self-confident place astonishing trust in their own abilities. Generally, they have a sense that they are in control of their lives, and have a firm belief in their capabilities that they will be able to achieve whatever they wish to. This, however, can be dangerous as it may lead to a build-up of over-confidence, which may negatively impact their self-worth and self-awareness. Individuals who are self-confident should learn to institute realistic expectations of things so that if a few of those expectations aren't met, they can still continue to remain positive and accept themselves for the way they are.

Parents have a responsibility to instill self-worth and self-awareness in their children. They can do this by helping their children realize their worth by pointing out their strengths and talents. If children are aware of these, it will more likely in turn boost their self-respect and self-confidence.

To be able to be successful in life, it is important for children to not look down upon themselves but to think of themselves positively, that they can do whatever they set out to achieve. However, parents need to make sure that their children don't end up being over-confident. They should not end up thinking that "Only I can do it"—that would be over-confidence. Rather they should think that "if I try my best, I will be able to do it"—this is self-confidence.

When your children fail to take appropriate action and do something that needs their attention, they might lose trust in their abilities and in themselves. This loss in faith can continue in a descending spiral that may cause failure in fulfilling their commitments. Here, parents will need to make their children understand that not everything in life will be sunny and rosy; there will be days when things just don't go as well as expected. However, children need to face such days with courage and confidence and not let this have an adverse effect on them, being de-motivating and making them question themselves and their capabilities.

Children should be assigned small tasks that may help in building a momentum and positive energy, which in turn will make other tasks easier to achieve. Once your children have built up their self-confidence and self-worth, they will be able to more willingly acknowledge more responsibility and even increase their capabilities as they become successful with new responsibilities.

Dependence vs. Independence

This might seem challenging, but to raise a child, you need to teach them to be independent, so that they can make decisions and be strong enough to face the world on their own. Also it is important to teach them to be dependent on others without having any sense of insecurity when they really need help.

Nowadays because of the increasingly fast-paced world lifestyle, many parents do not have as much time as they would like to give to their children. They may think they have ignored or even neglected their children to some degree. But it is important to find the time to teach your children how to be independent so that they don't always have to rely on you, and also how to be dependent when they genuinely need help and guidance from someone.

The society we live in today focuses a lot on making children completely independent, but this doesn't really work. Imagine that your child is a tree or a house, if the roots or the foundation is not right, won't that result in problems?

Attachment is extremely vital for the well-being of your children. Although evolutionary or historical practices are ways to attain this attachment, it is really about responsiveness. While refusing to comfort or feed your child or leave him to cry at certain times is non-responsive, you cannot simply spoil your baby by giving them too much love. Also you'll not create 'clingy children' or 'bad habits' by responding to them when they're in need. In reality, you'll be raising children who feel sufficiently secure to go outside and discover the world on their own, while knowing that they can return to a safe place if necessary.

Along with this, it is important that you allow your child to nurture his independence. Now, some parents have it backwards by giving too much freedom to their children when they are young, and then as they develop and yearn for more independence, they restrict it. You should permit children to explore. When they are at a younger age, this can be simply letting them climb up on a play structure on their own. However, as they get older, examples might be letting them go for walks or on bike rides to their friends' houses by themselves. You can always ensure that your child does something in the safest way possible, but if you completely eliminate their opportunities of practicing independence, even if out of fear that something wrong might happen, you will in effect be exploiting them.

If you give them the secure base of responsive parenting when they are young, they will know that they can always come to you when they need you.

Chapter 14: 4 Steps To Help Your Video Game "Addicted" Child

Computer addiction can include video games, online gambling, online pornography, chatting online and visiting different websites like social networking sites, forums, and online video streaming sites. Computer addiction can include the use of a smartphone, tablet, gaming console, laptop or desktop. Addiction has the potential to destroy relationships, work, and educational career opportunities. It can also lead to neglecting responsibilities as well as one's health. Computer addiction also has no boundaries in terms of sex, race, income, and age. Therefore, children are included in this issue. As a parent, how can we help our child break his or her addiction to computer devices?

Prohibit the use of the device to your child. As a parent, you have the authority to confiscate the device from your child. If the owner of the device is your child, hide it and lock it up in any closet or place that they cannot access without your permission. If you are the owner of the device, protect it with a password. You can even ask a favor of the parents of your child's friend to not to let your child use any computer device that his friend owns.

Provide them with alternative things to do. Same as the above explanation, provide the child with traditional toys, pets, or bond with your child outdoors. Playing sports with them and trying new things could end up being your guys' new hobby and can lead to many opportunities for socializing with friends and relatives.

Apply a reward method. It is hard for a child to understand why using the computer device is a bad thing to do, especially if the child only uses it for entertainment purposes. So if the child is in the process of detoxing, it is important to give the child rewards for their efforts of stopping the device use when they are told to do so.

Consult with a physician. Consulting with professionals is the best thing you can do as a parent because they know best in terms of this illness. Physicians that specialize in addiction can provide therapy to your addicted child. As a parent, try to ask the physician for advice on what things you possibly did wrong in parenting the child—since child addiction is always caused by irresponsible parenting.

Chapter 15: Train Your Child At An Early Age

RULE # 7 – Challenge Your Child's Thinking and Behavior

Raising great kids alone is challenging for single parents, but this can be possible if you train them early. Perhaps you have seen countless times how young children would cry when hungry or hurt. Before they think, they feel. Now, parents respond because they do not like hearing a baby cry. From the moment your child is born, he is wired to respond solely on how he feels. When he turns 1 and starts climbing stairs, even if you tell him the word "No!" he would still do it. This behavior is driven by his wants. So what do you do? You either encourage or quickly say "No". No matter how you handle this situation, what you need to know as a parent is that what is true when he is a toddler is still true when he reaches his teenage years. He will do what he wants to do. Just as a toddler wants to climb up stairs without even thinking the outcome when he falls is the same with a teenager who wants to drive fast without thinking that he might get into an accident.

From the moment your child starts thinking about what he wants to do, you may want to do the following:

Challenge his thinking and question his behavior. This way, when the time comes he is going to decide for himself, he will go to straight to you and ask, "Mom/Dad, is this really the right thing to do?" Your child knows what he feels, but ultimately, he knows that the final decision will still come from you.

Help your child find the balance between feelings and reason. Children and teenagers alike are mostly driven by their feelings and emotions. When faced with this kind of situation, it is best to train your child to seek you for decisions. He must be taught to respect your help and you must be the one to channel his emotions into useful avenues.

Teach him that a respectable adult should know how to feel and respond. You want your child to have intellectual wisdom, emotional depth, and mental prowess. None of them can be had without stimulating his thinking and training his behavior.

RULE # 8 – Provide a Set of Moral Guidelines

Children's capacity for rational thought is not yet fully developed even if they reach their teenage and early twenties. This is why the guidance of a sole parent is all the more important. The key to proper communication with your children is not just through listening, but you must also be clear about your expectations of them. Do no not send them mixed messages. You must set clear guidelines at the very beginning and must also be a good example to your child.

To do this, you need to first think of moral guidelines you would want to instill in your child so that you will raise him to be the kind of kid you want him to be. Lying should not be an option, so never ask him to tell the credit card company that you are not home. Never use curse words in the house if you do not want him to use them as well. Be respectful when talking to elders if you want them to follow suit. Children watch what you do and follow what you say. So always be on the lookout should you be pushed off the moral fence.

Finally, when you impose your set of moral guidelines, make sure that he sees your leadership and conviction. This will help strengthen him to be his own person someday. Lack of moral guidelines set by parents may result in your child just going with the flow and with what the majority dictates. He will not have a mind of his own and would assume that his unexamined thoughts are automatically acceptable.

RULE # 9 – Do Not Blur the Lines between Right and Wrong

Simply put, what is right should always be right and what is wrong should never be partly right. One of the most common mistakes single parents make when raising kids alone is they often rationalize bad behavior, normalize the bizarre, and even tolerate disrespect and dishonesty. As a parent, it is acceptable that you wanted to give everything to your kids and approved of their every request, but make sure that you do not confuse what is right from wrong behavior. You cannot just allow your child to risk his future just because you cannot confront him of issues in school, with his friends, and other extracurricular activities.

When you suspect that your child is bullying his classmate or asking them for food, but lets it slide because you cannot be with him all the time or he might get offended when you try opening up this discussion, if you suspect your 15-year old of smoking and just let the situation pass and "at least he is not into drugs", if you let your teenage girl have boyfriend at such an early age and does not confront her for not telling you or "at least she is not pregnant", it might look as if you child wins all the time.

To be a parent means to play as the leader, to be ahead of them when they walk, to intervene, to instruct, and be the strong foundation in forming his character so he will know how to distinguish right from wrong. If you keep on letting things pass and blurring the reality that wrong is indeed wrong, you will eventually fail raising a great kid. Your kid needs a parent that will tell things straight to the point and yet still love and support them all the way provided that everything is in accordance to your moral standards.

Chapter 16: Tips On Awareness

The teenage era is a total of 7 years. Therefore, it is expected that there are more tips needed to survive those long seven years. Here are additional tips you could use.

1. Be on the look out for danger signs.

Although they have good judgment they are still human, they are prone to make mistakes. Even with proper guidance, teens can do so many foolish things. Teenagers may not approach about their problems for fear of you getting angry or fear of embarrassment. Do not take lightly the changes that you see in your teen, if you feel that they are destructive for him or her.

Professional help may be needed. If there are sudden occurrences of inappropriate things like a drastic change in personality, failing grades, symptoms of drug or substance abuse, sleep problems, or comments about suicide or the like, take immediate action before it is too late.

2. Be aware of what your teens watch, hear, do, and play on the internet.

The latest technology can sometimes be the cause of many problems. Be hands-on parents. Place the computer in a place where there are others who could see them. Limit the use and access to Internet. Inform the teens of the different dangers they could encounter in not practicing safe internet use.

Encourage your teen to spend more time outside of cyberspace. They could join outdoor activities or volunteer for worthy causes. The number of problems arising from the teenage years has increased with the emergence of online social media and games. Protect your teenagers from themselves and other people as well. Constant monitoring and will help.

3. Respect your teen's privacy.

Unless you suspect something detrimental is going on in your teen's life, you must respect his or her privacy too. This is very hard for parents to do. They sometimes snoop in their teens' rooms, cell phones, diaries, emails, or other social networks as a way of "checking" on their kids. They sometimes stalk their teens. Trust is a big word. Let your teens know that you do trust them and that you can also be trusted. At this time, they tend to be very secretive. As long as you don't notice any alarming changes in your teens, leave them room for growth on their own. You do not need to know everything about your teen. You do not have to discover all their secrets.

Chapter 17: Role Of Communication In Handling Teen Kids

Having clear communication and expression would really woo your teenager. Youngsters love to develop values, ideas, and beliefs that may not be as same as of yours. This is a part of the normal process of steering them towards independence. Prepare yourself with one fact that communication with teenagers is going to be different from communicating with younger children and may involve some conflicts.

For conducive and communicative parenting, follow these suggestions –

ü Take joint decisions and discuss issues with clear intention to leave the arguments behind.

ü Teenagers are certainly going to have viewpoints alien to yours or that you won't understand. Train your mind to see good in their standpoint.

ü Whenever your teen kid acts wrong or careless, be supportive. They will learn valuable lessons from their mistakes.

ü Love them unconditionally and listen to them a lot. Offer to take them to or pick them up from places.

ü As a conscious parent, give them enough privacy. Teenagers deserve to have their own space. Don't forget to knock going into their room. They would really appreciate this gesture.

- Your teenage kid may be struggling with their changing sense of identity and need to feel loved. Speak loving words and demonstrate your love.

- Celebrate their achievements and forgive their mistakes. Show interest in them to make them feel included. This would really boost their self-esteem.

- Yelling, nagging, and harsh criticism is a big no-no. Refrain from negative communication where you may criticize them for trying harder. Also, be selective over argumentative topics. Even criticism should be constructive.

- If you are wrong some ways, apologize. This will teach them a million dollar lesson.

ü Think carefully before saying 'no' to their request. Your negation should accompany reason. Simply forget the parental clichés that may invite tension.

ü Don't underestimate the power of listening. Your teenage kid with happily confide in once they get convinced that they are really being listened to.

ü There is always a way to say. Instead of saying 'Don't act irresponsibly' or 'You never tell me your whereabouts'. Instead frame your sentences like 'If I know your whereabouts, I would worry less'. Just minus sarcasm from your sarcasm.

Get Smarter and Savvier

Make your parenting not just conscious but even smarter and savvier. Don't look muted or dumbwhen your young kids talk about the latest gadgets. It is time to have an understanding of the technology that drives the teenagers' lives.

Learn about your teenager's cyber space hangouts. Set up your own accounts and experience bonding. Also discuss with them about cyber safety to make them realize they're not in some online mess.

Keep a Track and Not Spy

Yeah...there is a slim gap between tracking and spying. You have to make them understand that you intend to ensure their safety and not just disturb. Remind your teen not to share his passwords, even with a best friend. Talk about the bad situations that can arise from sharing passwords.

Chapter 18: Transition To Elementary School For Your Child

Preschool (elementary school) is one of the most important stages of a child's school life. At first the child is excited that she will be going to school, but as time goes by, she becomes reluctant and does not want school anymore.

When a kid goes to a new school, it is filled with unfamiliar faces of teachers and fellow students. She also realizes that there is a set of rules and regulations to be followed. This may cause a lot of anxiety and anticipation. The child experiences mixed feelings and do not know how to react to this changes.

When I joined elementary school, our teacher showed us where the toilets were and what we were supposed to say so as to be allowed to use them. However, I could not face the teacher to ask her to allow using the toilets. I was afraid of her so I ended up urinating on myself. I am sure most of the parents will identify with such kind of behavior.

Here are some things you can do to ensure that your child has an easier time;

Having fun as you prepare for preparatory school

So now its a few weeks before your child joins preschool. There are a lot of activities you can do to make her look forward to joining. However, these activities should be done in moderation to ensure she does not end up being afraid instead of being excited.

·Try the idea of role playing to explore elementary school

Take turns to play the role of teacher, parents and the student. The activities should involve saying goodbye to mom and/or dad, singing songs, scribbling and reading books. Reassure your kid that school will be fun and that she will make new friends. If she has any questions, make sure you answer them patiently. It will help make the anxiety less and she will feel in control of the situation.

·Take time to read elementary school books

Try to read books that are familiar with those your child will read when she goes to elementary school. Read out the story and ask for her view on the characters.

·Teach her things she should do for herself teach her things like carrying her backpack, fastening her shoe laces, opening her lunch box, zipping her coat and putting on her pullover. You can make it fun like you ask her to pack picnic food stuffs. That way she will be able to carry her back pack, open her lunch box and make sure she puts on shoes with laces.

·Familiarize with her new school take her to her new school and ask for permission to take a tour. This will boost her confidence and increase her comfort in the new environment.

·Take time to listen to what her worries are despite all these things, you have to listen to what her worries might be. They may be small or big but they will greatly affect her if you do not listen to her.

Assure your youngster that it is okay to feel afraid, frightened, dismayed and stressed.

You can give her an example of a time you felt the same way and how you overcame it.

·Read the child's nonverbal cues your child may not be able to express everything she feels by word of mouth. You may realize that even though your child did not have any problems in potty training, she gets an accident. These are signs that your child is stressed.

You may also find that your child becomes aggressive, clingy, withdrawn or start throwing tantrums. Take it easy and help her overcome her anxiety.

Chapter 19: Do Not Overstep Your Bounds

Not overstepping your bounds simply means that you should not disrespect your spouse's wishes when it comes to the treatment of his/her children. If for some reason, you and your spouse have not discussed and agreed on the parenting/step parenting roles, you must NOT take on the authoritarian role with your step child.

Does this mean that you ignore your step child if he or she is misbehaving? No, it does not! It means that you should remove the child from the situation and put him or her in a safe "holding cell" until the natural parent returns.

You need to establish yourself as a responsible adult who is going to uphold the rules of the family/household. You should never ignore unacceptable behavior from ANY child in your home. But you must learn how to exercise your power in an appropriate way. If the child is older than 9 or 10, sending him/her to his/her bedroom is appropriate discipline for the moment.

But do not send the child to his/her room until you have sat down and discussed the misbehavior with him or her. You do want to be involved in the punishment at this time, but you want the punishment or consequences to be a unified decision. This shows the child or children that you and your spouse are a united front when it comes to their behavior and adhering to the family rules. This will go a long way in you not ending up being the wicked step parent.

Parenting is not a one man band appearance. You are in this together. If you share in the responsibility together, you will earn the respect and love of your children. There should always be a sit-down meeting of both parents with the child who is being disciplined, where you explain the action and the implications and consequences of it. There should never be a response of "because I said so" or because "I am the boss." Children need to know why whatever they did is wrong. This is how they learn appropriate behavior. Their slate is clean—you need to be the one to write on it.

Interestingly enough, this rule should be followed by all parents, not just step parents. Children should never be placed in the position of being able to play one parent against the other. Co-parenting involves both parents to be on the same page; this teaches the child responsibility and fairness.

Above all, do not strike or spank your step children. No parent should ever strike a child! What kind of lesson does that teach children? Will they think it is okay to hit others if they do wrong? Does it open a door for them to be bullies? Is violence a way to make things right? These are questions that all parents should ask themselves before they decide to spank or hit their children.

This also includes the opposite end of the stick too: giving your step children freedoms without discussing the situation with their natural parents. Sometimes step parents want to be the nice guy—the good cop/bad cop situation. They want to be "friends" with the kids and they will let them do things that perhaps they should not be doing, without checking with their partner first. This again will send the message that you and your spouse are not a united team, and it will set up the ability for the kids to play one parent against the other. Not only is this situation bad for the family, but it is a killer to your marriage.

Many marriages end because of parenting issues. That is why it is so important for the couple to discuss and agree on their parenting styles BEFORE they marry. It will save everyone in the family a lot of heartache in the end. As parents, we are responsible for the healthy teaching of our children and helping them to grow up to be good responsible adults. Hillary Clinton said that it takes a village...but it certainly begins with the two parents who set the strongest example for them to follow in their home.

Chapter 20: Newborn To 23 Months

In the last chapter, we painted a pretty picture of mother and newborn baby gazing into each other's eyes, sunk into an oxytocin moment of peace and connection. Of course, it's not always that way.

Society sees women as "natural-born mothers." Women supposedly have an innate desire to mother, and an effortless competence at it. And certainly, the oxytocin released during childbirth and breastfeeding can make mothering seem like the most natural thing in the world to some women.

However, it's not uncommon for a new mother to feel anxious or indifferent when confronted with this little stranger. Whether you gave birth to or adopted this baby, although you've been preparing for months or even years, it may be hard to merge the feelings you've developed for the baby of your imagination with this very real human being who's suddenly appeared.

Becoming a parent, whether by giving birth or via adoption, triggers any fears you have about intimacy and love. Just as you're beginning to shape your baby's ability to love by the way you nurture her, so your own oxytocin response was shaped by your own parents' style of nurturing.

As we discussed in Chapter 2, if you didn't receive Oxytocin Parenting when you were a child, you'll have to be careful not to pass on learned tendencies to react with fear. On the other hand, opening up to love with a baby is a wonderful way to expand your own capacity to love.

So, don't be concerned if you find yourself taking those first steps after the baby has arrived.

The simple acts of physically caring for the baby can activate your oxytocin response. Your bond with your baby will continue to build over the first few days, weeks or even months of her life.

Remember, at this period you are setting the brain's emotional thermostat: shaping her stress response and her oxytocin response. The most important activities for Oxytocin Parenting at this stage are also the most obvious and natural: feeding and touching.

What's Happening in Your Baby's Brain?

You know how a child's cognitive abilities develop over time. Each milestone, such as sitting up, crawling, talking or toilet training, builds on previous development.

Your child's emotional development runs on a parallel course, and it too builds on previous steps.

At the newborn stage, you begin to build your baby's basic sense of security and trust. Positive experiences of comfort and nurture encourage the spread of oxytocin receptors in the brain.

At the same time, the amygdala, or fear center, continues to develop. It's normal and inevitable that your baby will experience anxiety and fear. Your goal as an Oxytocin Parent is to make sure that safety and love experiences outweigh fear experiences — that's all.

At about two months, your baby will begin to smile when she looks at you. This is a crucial period, because it establishes the connection in your baby's brain between positive emotion and another person. At around two months, your baby will move from simple attention to active emotion. His attention may seem more focused as you look into each other's eyes, and he may coo or make other positive noises.

During this period, you really begin to build the attachment between you, as emotion becomes more reciprocal. As you gaze into each other's eyes, make faces and smile at each other, the baby is learning how to communicate positive emotion through expression. Your infant may seem more responsive, and this makes it more fun to interact with him.

Your baby experiences this, too. His brain associates the pleasure of looking at you with good physical feelings, and every time you interact, this association becomes reinforced. Your attention becomes more and more pleasurable and important to him, and it becomes the basis for your stable, loving relationship.

This positive feedback loop is building his oxytocin response. His brain begins to release oxytocin when he looks at you, creating a strong association between you and pleasure — and this will become a neural habit. His brain cells wire themselves into a circuit that he'll use for all kinds of positive social interactions.

Feed the emotions, as well as the body

The most important bonding activity for both of you is feeding. It's about much more than nutrition. Feeding is a baby's first experience of nurturing, and the flow of oxytocin from the mother's body to the baby's may be his first experience of the oxytocin response.

In Bonding, Marshall Klaus, John Kennell and Phyllis Klaus describe the actions of a newborn if he's placed on his mother's belly instead of being taken away for cleaning or medical procedures will in the first hour of life. He quickly finds his way to her nipple and begins to suckle. (This process was first observed by a team that included Kerstin Uvnas-Moberg.) The suckling increases the mother's release of oxytocin, causing her milk to let down; it's likely that it also increases the effects of oxytocin in her brain, causing the positive feedback loop.

As the milk begins to flow into the baby's stomach, it causes the release of CCK, a digestive chemical that signals the brain to release oxytocin into the bloodstream. It's probable that the baby's brain also fills with oxytocin, which begins the bonding process with his mother.

Every time she nurses him, strokes him, gazes into his eyes, she's building the oxytocin response. His brain is learning that another person — this one special person — is a reliable source of comfort and pleasure. He also comes to expect that his physical needs will be met. He'll be safe, secure, warm and protected.

Your pediatrician will no doubt give you plenty of information about how much to feed your newborn, and about how fast his body should be growing. But providing his nutritional needs is far from the whole story. One of the key concepts of Oxytocin Parenting is feeding to build attachment by triggering the oxytocin response.

Think of feeding in two parts. One part is the providing of food to your baby, whether you're breast- or bottle-feeding. The other part is the close physical contact as you hold her close to your heart. Babies who are bottle-fed may miss the sensory contact with mommy's breast, but you still can cradle her against your breast as you feed her — and this is at least as critical as actually getting sustenance into her.

You may not always be able to drop everything for a feeding session, but avoid getting into the habit of bottle-propping while you feed the baby. There are products on the market designed to hold the bottle comfortably and securely so you can do other things. But bottle-propping is dangerous for two reasons: First, it's all too easy for your baby to choke; this is a life-threatening situation. Second, it short-circuits the brain development linking sensory pleasure and emotional comfort that your newborn should be developing.

Also resist the temptation to multi-task. You may feel like you can't get anything else done while your baby is eating every two to four hours. Your arm may get tired. It may be irresistible to take a phone call

— especially if you can use your mobile phone's headset anyway. But your baby needs you to be present and involved in her feeding.

Remember how the baby's stomach releases CCK when it's digesting milk? This seems to be an essential part of the bonding process. When oxytocin researcher Kerstin Uvnas-Moberg blocked the effects of CCK in baby sheep, they lost the ability to recognize their mothers.

You're probably aware of the way baby geese and ducks imprint on the first being they see after they're born. Humans, with our more flexible brains, may not have such a strong and sudden imprinting, but it's likely that a similar process of imprinting takes place during feeding. One of the effects of oxytocin in the brain is to tie positive experiences to individuals: We remember who we love and seek to be with them.

As your newborn's brain begins to associate the reward of food with attachment to you, you are imprinting his brain with the pattern for love.

Touching Your Baby

If touch is so important, why do we tend to be stingy with this special gift to our babies? The skin is the largest organ of the body and one of the most direct sources of stimulation to the brain. Unfortunately, this is a two-way street. To give touch is also to receive it.

If a parent isn't used to touch, feels immune to touch, or has experienced touch in a negative way in the past, such as from abuse, that parent will unwittingly avoid affectionate touch with the baby to avoid the unconscious triggers that it creates. Additionally, if a parent is already stressed, the addition of touch combined with the crying of the baby or demand to nurse is more than he or she can handle.

The other challenge to touch and affection is the constant negative reinforcement of the medical establishment's views on spoiling children and the pressures we're given to instill independence in children as early as possible. You cannot spoil a child by holding him too much. This is physiologically impossible. You can only spoil a child through material overindulgence which becomes a substitute for your presence and involvement.

Arms, not furniture

Many of the tools and tips that are provided to parents at the earliest stages of their baby's vital brain development are contrary to optimal emotional health and development. A few of these are bottles, pacifiers, baby carriers, strollers, and cribs. These very common things create obstacles to secure attachment and bonding with our children.

Bottles are encouraged from the beginning, as are pacifiers. Often, we view feeding our children as a mere necessity to sustaining life, but breastfeeding is about more than just providing nutrients. It also provides eye-to-eye and skin-to-skin contact, the sound of the heartbeat, the smell of the mother, and the matching of body temperatures. All of these sensory experiences have direct brain-altering effects, and they all generate a tremendous oxytocin response, providing the baby with sustained and prolonged soothing which enables the regulation of emotions. Unfortunately, many of us grew up on a bottle, so giving it to our child becomes second nature that is nearly hereditary.

The natural barrier created by the bottle grows when we prop the bottle, avoiding all contact, and the pacifier that's given with every cry or whine prevents the much needed oxytocin response brought about by pleasant parent/child exchanges.

Baby carriers, strollers, and cribs are additional obstacles to the attachment bond because they enable further disconnection. In some tribal cultures where carrying the baby is commonplace for up to three years and beyond, parents become so attuned and sensitive to their child's experience that they can predict exactly when the child is about to relieve himself.

In our culture, we constantly look for ways to make parenting easier while failing to understand that artificial parenting tools deprive our babies of the natural soothing sensory experiences that they need. When you walk with, carry, hold, sling, or swing your child, you generate necessary soothing experiences for your baby's brain during these critical stages of development.

Certainly, you will use a stroller, carrier, crib and bottle — and don't feel guilty about it. Just remember that the more times you touch, hold and carry your baby, the more oxytocin you share.

Action Steps for birth through 18 months

The following practices don't need to be done all the time or even every day. But each of them will help make up for the times you can't be physically connected with your baby.

1. Sleep with your baby. The family bed is a very important way to connect with your child if you must be absent from him during the course of a day. Research has demonstrated how bed-sharing brings all members into physiological alignment, contributing to improved relating, attunement, and need-meeting. In her book, Attachment Parenting, Katie Granju notes: "Babies usually sleep better, as well as children. Parents sleep better. Night feeding and nursing is made easier. It provides built in snuggle time for the father, teaches babies that nighttime is for sleeping, and it also can make up for a hard day."

2. Bathe with your baby. A warm tub simulates the womb. For many babies, this was a pleasant and oxytocin-rich time. Spending time in a warm bath with your baby is an excellent way to create soothing for both of you.

3. Massage your baby. While lying in bed or on the floor, take deep breaths – inhaling and exhaling – as you stroke your baby's body gently using baby-sensitive oil or lotion. Think positive thoughts, and speak positive words. Turn him over, and gaze into his eyes as you stroke his arms, tummy, head, legs, and feet very gently. Permit him to gaze into your eyes. This is a powerful attachment and bonding experience.

4. Sling your baby. When you can, put your baby in a sling, facing toward you as you walk around the house, do chores, and go for walks. (Facing babies outward away from your body before they're neurologically developed enough to handle all of the stimulation is a common sling mistake. There is far too much sensory stimulation for a baby to manage at this young age while facing out. When she faces toward you, the bouncing and

contact with your body soothes her brain, stimulates positive hormone changes, and helps her body's rhythms sync with yours.

5. Gaze into your baby's eyes. Breastfeeding simply isn't always practical. When bottle feeding, hold him in your arms with eye-to-eye contact. If possible, get skin-to-skin contact with your baby by moving aside some of his and your clothing. Make eye contact, and sing, hum or talk as you give the bottle.

What If My Baby Is in Daycare?

More than half of working women in the U.S. have a child under a year old. If you're among this majority, you may wonder, "Will my baby love her care provider more than she loves me?" Or, "Will she be able to develop a strong oxytocin response if she's in daycare?"

A national study of the effects of childcare on children from infants to kindergarten found that babies formed insecure attachments only when a mother had "low levels of sensitivity" when interacting with her baby and the baby received poor-quality daycare. (This study did find that more time in daycare translated into more problem behaviors, like arguing a lot, between two- and four-and-a-half-year-olds.)

On the other hand, children who spent time in daycare programs that provided enrichment and learning activities actually showed better language and cognitive development than kids who were cared for at home.

In any case, the study found that the home environment — the characteristics of the parents and the family — were more strongly linked to a child's development than were the features of childcare.

Focus on Oxytocin Parenting during whatever period of family leave you can take and continue to provide Oxytocin Parenting as much as you can when you're home with your baby.

If you come home from work upset or exhausted, you must learn to calm and settle your own stress reactions following a difficult day away from your baby. Upon returning home, be willing to spend uninterrupted time reconnecting and regulating your baby. Your baby will experience significant stress when you're away, but you can repair this rapidly by making skin-to-skin connection.

Chapter 21: Positive Parenting With Teenagers

We have now reached the chapter that is just about as comparable at times to the terrible twos of toddlerhood: the teen years. Your once small baby has grown up into a young adult, and they certainly let you know this, too. Parenting a teenager can be quite tricky, for they are out and about in the big ole scary world, led by a brain that has not quite matured yet. This can be scary for any parent, making them want to keep their teen kid locked up in the house. This chapter will discuss some great methods to keep in mind as you learn to properly parent a teenager.

Teenagers want to make their own decisions. We were all teens once, we know this feeling. It is natural. But it's important to remember that the teenage brain still has quite a bit of developing to do. It is also natural as a parent to not trust the judgment of your teenage child. During this time, teens become more acquainted with their peers rather than their parents, which is why establishing a grounded family life is vital to staying connected to your maturing teenager. When early parenthood is done correctly, you will continue to stay invested in your teen's life, and may even be rehired as their advisor or friend. If you do a superb job, your teen will more than likely listen to the advice you give them.

The media has really ruined the image of a teenager. They typically are always playing the role as defiant, sassy, snotty mini-adults that think they know it all and can rule the world. While there are those teens out there, the ones who are responsible, live by good judgment, and are considerate of others are out there, too. The problem parents have with raising teens is that they no longer feel like they have much of an influence on their child. On the contrary, their behavior is actually a direct correlation to the bond they have with their parental figures.

You're Their Parent, AND Their Friend

Teens, no matter what they try to make you believe, crave the knowledge of knowing their parents understand them and will love them no matter what. This is where forming a type of friendship is vital. But many parents can become overbearing, and this turns off a teen from their parents faster than you can answer a doorbell. Teens need their independence, which can make parents feel shut out of their lives. But don't fret! They will be more open to talking to you about things if you accept that they require the independence to learn.

More often than not, if you give your teenager the consideration and respect they too deserve, they are more likely to dish it back to your as their parent in return. But don't let this keep you from saying no to certain things. You teenager still needs boundaries, and whether they want to admit it or not, they are looking to you to set them.

Establish Time Together

As a parent of a teenager, make the time to check in with them each and every day. Just a few minutes of communication at the dinner table or while you pick up the house before its time for bed can help to establish a path of open communication. This is SO important. Most teenagers still like their parents giving them a good-night hug and appreciate when you check in with them to see how they are and how their day was. Also, I recommend setting up a time at least once a week to do something special with your teenage child. Going on a walk or getting a snack at their favorite restaurant will suffice.

Actively but Appropriately Parent

Don't refuse to acknowledge that your child is maturing. This will only invite rebellion into your household, which is fun for no one in the family. Teenagers need more freedom. Ask where they are going and who they are hanging out with. An important part of parenting a teen is getting to know their friends as well as their parents so that you are familiar with regular activities.

Have High Standards

Your teenagers want to strive to be the best they can be. As their parent, support your teen and their decisions. Do not intrude on them achieving goals and in their decision making. They need to make and chart their goals now so that they successfully can as adults. Support the passions your teen has and allow them to explore the world. It is important at this age that they find their own voice.

Eat Meals Together

I highly recommend making this a priority for the entire family. Family dinner time is an opportune time to sit down, enjoy a good meal, and listen to how everyone's day/week is going. It's also much easier to spot potential arising issues when you can see your teen's reactions to questions.

Keep Up Lines of Communication

If you lose an open communication line, you as a parent will totally lose sight of what is occurring in your teen's life, which means you will lose all control of influencing any sort of outcome.

Encourage Self-Care

Just like in younger kids, you need to keep up the limitations when it comes to your teen caring for themselves. This means encourage them to get plenty of rest and to eat healthy. Their minds and bodies are still growing and need adequate nutrients to be strong and healthy. Coffee is not a great idea for teens, since it can greatly affect their sleeping patterns. Set some sort of rule to put away all mobile devices before bed, since this can affect sleep too.

Conduct Regular Family Meetings

The purpose of family get-togethers is to provide a type of forum to everyone in the family to talk about disagreements, schedules, and any other concerns. This also is a good forum to lay down ground rules. Give everyone a chance to speak without interruptions and encourage positive feedback. For teenagers, I have found that adding in incentives like ice cream or pizza helps them want to join in on the conversation.

Keep Computers in a Common Space in the House

We have all seen those movies where teenagers are being majorly cyber-bullied by peers at school while the parents remain oblivious to anything happening. To keep this from happening to your teenager, place the computer in a common spit in the house. This includes laptops as well. It is difficult to track what your teens do while online. With it being located in an area where anyone can see what they are doing, they will be far less likely to venture into things they know they are not supposed to get into, etc.

Don't Push Independence before They are Ready

Just like all humans, every single teenager is different in how they blossom from a young child into a maturing young adult. The definition of real independence should include close relationships with other people, but should never include the feeling of rebellion. Do not push your child into independence. Respect their personal time table.

Make Agreements for Repair

If you have used positive parenting skills throughout their childhood, your teenager will be far less likely to damage the trust between you. This means they more than likely won't be dishonest and they won't want to step beyond the boundaries you have set for them. If they do happen to step on your toes, ask them how they plan to repair the damage and trust broken.

Make Staying Connected a Priority as They Venture into the Real World

As a parent, it is difficult but you must be willing to accept your child's dependency. They are their own separate person now, which means as a parent you must strive to keep connected with them as they live through high school and discover who they are as a unique individual. It is natural for teens to want to spend more time with peers and friends than with their parents. Teens who were raised in a well-grounded household that utilized positive parenting skills will respond well to the efforts that parents use to stay connected. As a parent, it is your responsibility to keep up the job of your teen's moral and emotional compass. Kids at this age will be experimenting with relationships that are outside of the family.

You should invite your teen to rely on you emotionally until they can depend on themselves. I see in our culture frequently that we let teens put their dependency on people and things that are outside the family circle, which can result in disastrous, complicated situations.

Conclusion

In our discussion, it is clear that the ultimate gift you can give your child is a sense of responsibility and discipline. To achieve this, our unconditional love, patience and care should be the first priority to our children after which you will be able to apply Zen mindful steps. In summary, the steps are right understanding, right intentions, right actions, meditation, mindfulness, effort, right livelihood, and right speech. Embracing all these steps is what will make the difference between your child growing up into a responsible adult or not. Even as you begin the journey on Zen parenting, remember that it will be hard to change the way you are used to parenting your child. However, with a little more practice, you will use Zen to instill discipline and responsibility and you will be happy when your children grow up to become responsible adults.

www.ingramcontent.com/pod-product-compliance
Lightning Source LLC
Chambersburg PA
CBHW052204090526
44583CB00015BA/1326